THE
LORD'S PRAYER

ALSO BY E. F. SCOTT

**MAN AND SOCIETY
IN THE
NEW TESTAMENT**
Published by Charles Scribner's Sons

ERNEST FINDLAY SCOTT is widely known as the author of many outstanding religious books, among them, *The Nature of the Early Church, The Book of Revelation, Literature of the New Testament, The Purpose of the Gospels.* Born in England, he studied at Glasgow, Oxford, and the United Presbyterian College in Edinburgh before accepting professorships successively at Queen's University in Canada and at Union Theological Seminary in New York. Dr. Scott died in 1954.

THE
LORD'S PRAYER

ITS CHARACTER, PURPOSE, AND INTERPRETATION

BY

E. F. SCOTT, D.D.

CHARLES SCRIBNER'S SONS, NEW YORK

PREFACE

IT IS NOT A LITTLE REMARKABLE that among the countless books on early Christianity there is hardly one which deals solely, and from a critical and historical point of view, with the Lord's Prayer. This, when all is said, is the primary Christian document, and the only one which comes directly from Jesus himself. We are often reminded that he wrote nothing, and that all we know of his message is through the reports of others. But he was himself the author of this prayer, and took care to write it indelibly on the memories of his disciples. In the attempt to discover what he taught we can go behind all traditions to this clear statement, signed, as it were, with his own hand. The prayer is so familiar that we have come to take it for granted, like the ground we stand on or the air we breathe, and this is no doubt the reason that it has been so little investigated. But as soon as we fix our minds on it we are faced by many questions which require an answer. Why did Jesus make it? How did it differ from all previous prayers? How are its various parts related to one another? What is involved in the petitions when they are taken together and one by one?

What evidence do they afford us of Jesus' mode of thinking, and of his attitude to God and man? It was one of his main intentions that those who said his prayer should reflect on it. He saw that the act of prayer in his time had often become little more than a pious gesture, mechanically performed, and that men were thus losing all vital contact with God. His object was to frame a prayer which did not consist of formal words but which would compel men to think of what they said. For this reason it is composed of short sentences with pauses between them in which the mind might react on the words spoken. It has to be confessed that his own prayer, like those which he condemned, has become a matter of "vain repetition" for the great majority even of devout Christians. There is nothing which would help so much to put new life into our religion than an effort to understand the Lord's Prayer while we repeat it. I offer this book in the hope that it may contribute in some little measure towards this end.

E. F. Scott.

CONTENTS

vii

THE
LORD'S PRAYER

CHAPTER I

JESUS' CONCEPTION OF PRAYER

THE Lord's Prayer has come to us from Jesus himself, and has always lain at the very heart of his religion. Churches have differed widely in every matter of doctrine and ritual and government, but all unite in the Lord's Prayer. There has never been a time when it was not daily repeated by all Christians, alike in their common worship and their private devotion. It is the watchword by which they recognise each other, whatever may be their race or calling or their plane of culture. They learn it as children and hold fast to it, through all changing experiences, until they die.

It has this abiding quality because it is no mere statement of belief but a prayer, and prayer is the vital thing in religion. Everything else that may enter into our service of God, sacrifices and holy days, music and art and pious custom, is meant only to accompany prayer or to present it in another form. Not only in acts of worship but in all righteous living, in all seeking after truth, men are unconsciously praying to God, in the hope that he will answer them. "To work is to pray" was the motto of the ancient monks. "Thinking is prayer" said the philosopher, when his religion was called

1

in question. Michelangelo defended his love of beauty in the same manner: "I am trying," he said, "to make a perfect thing, and that is prayer, for God is perfection, and I am seeking him." So it was not by accident that this prayer of Jesus was singled out from his sayings as that which explained all the others. He had given a new religion, and religion in its essence is prayer. It was therefore in the prayer he taught his disciples that men found the substance of his message.

His prayer was a new one, but there has never been a time when men have not prayed. Their conceptions of God have often been crude and childish. Their interests have been limited to some little tribe, and to their struggle for bare existence. Yet in its fundamental character prayer has always been the same, for it springs out of the primal necessities of human nature. Men cannot live together unless they can communicate their needs to one another, and therefore they learned to speak. They were conscious also of a higher power on which their lives depended, and they were impelled to speak to God, as they did to their fellow-men. This was the origin of prayer, and perhaps it was first employed merely to own the presence of an invisible power. The earliest prayers are little more than expressions of awe before the mysterious forces with which man's life is surrounded, and which might crush him if they were not appeased and honoured. But along with this reverence for the higher power there grew up the sense that it might be won over to man's side. To all appearance it was indifferent to him and often cruel and capricious. But it might be moved to help him if it was approached with gifts and offerings, accompanied by urgent prayers.

As far back as we can go men thought of the unknown power as in some way related to themselves. They pictured the gods as magnified men, actuated by motives and passions similar to their own, and this has often been attributed to the childish character of all primitive thinking. This cannot, however, be the whole explanation. We still believe in a correspondence of the human mind with the great order of nature, and this is no childish belief. All our science is grounded on it. The highest task of the poet and the thinker is to make it real to us. Man, as the Greek philosopher declared, is the measure of all things. By the mind in himself he is in sympathy with the universal mind. In the primitive myths we can discern man's first stammering efforts to express his sense of his own affinity with the divine. It was this sense which made prayer possible. No one would ever think of praying to an earthquake or a hurricane or the law of gravitation. But man was conscious of something that was behind these blind forces and controlled them—something that was akin to himself.

It was also involved in the very idea of prayer that the higher power was beneficent. In the savage religions and in the worship of Baal and Moloch there seems to be little anticipation of the Christian confidence in the love of God. But the fact remains that even in those religions men prayed. They could never have done so unless they believed that their god, however terrible his aspect, might be moved to pity. They must have felt, however obscurely, that the divine power must ultimately be one of goodness, and that amidst the calamities of life they could look to it for help and deliverance. Prayer had its origin in this unquenchable trust in God. From all the hostile forces which threatened to overwhelm them men made their appeal to God, assured that he was merciful.

The chief object of prayer has always been to ask for something. Usually it has been for a material benefit, a plenteous harvest, recovery from sickness, victory in battle, success in a dangerous enterprise. The ancient prayers which have come down to us seldom rise above this level, and the same is true of most of our prayers today. But in all periods there has been at least some glimmering of other gifts which are at God's disposal, and which may be obtained by prayer. Men feel that they have sinned against him and wish to be forgiven. They have need of wisdom and strength of purpose, of power to resist not only outward enemies but their own base passions. They pray on behalf of others as well as for themselves. They look beyond immediate interests to those which concern their higher welfare. Not only so, but they conjoin their prayer with thanksgiving. It must never be forgotten that even in the earliest times this was an essential element in prayer. To beg new favours from God was not enough. You needed to remember what he had already done for you and to assure him that you were grateful. The motive may partly have been to persuade him that having done so much he might do more, but even so prayer had to be accompanied with gratitude. Men were to ask of God because they had learned to trust him. They appealed to him in their present need because they had found him to be just and merciful.

Prayer, therefore, even in its crudest forms, was much more than a begging for supernatural aid. It was the acknowledgment of a power above, which men could rely on in their earthly weakness. It enabled them to live reverently, ever mindful of the higher power. It was a means not only of seeking God's favour, but of consulting with him. Before acting for yourself you laid the matter before God. To be sure you wished him to do what you desired, but you referred your own plan to his judgment and by doing so were compelled to see it from the higher point of view. If you felt that he condemned it you could draw back; if you could be certain that he approved it you could go forward confidently. This has always been one of the chief purposes of prayer. Taking God into our counsels we gain a calmer and wider vision, and men were conscious in the remotest times, as we are now, that prayer had this effect. "Come and let us reason together, saith the Lord." The prophet here expresses what has always been in men's minds when they sincerely prayed.

Nevertheless the primary aim was to receive some gift from God, and it has often been held that in this respect prayer is only the survival of a primitive error. In so far as it implies trust in God and the sense of dependence on him it indeed has its roots in all that it is deepest in our nature. But why approach him with those constant requests for things that we want? A child has this habit of always asking, and we try to cure him of it. He must not expect every whim to be gratified; he must be content with his own share; he must learn to do things for himself instead of leaning on others. In early times, we are told, men were like children, always asking God to help them. We must now act like full-grown men, and take responsibility for our lives. God has given us faculties and opportunities, and requires that we should use them. Prayer is weakening, and instead of beseeching him to act for us we should act for ourselves.

It is argued, too, that prayer is presumptuous in so far as it seeks to change or in some manner to influence the mind of God. He has established the world's order and is shaping our destiny as he sees best. We try by prayer to interfere with his purposes, to deflect him from his own course into another which will be more pleasing to ourselves. We wish him, moreover, to discriminate in our favour, relaxing on our behalf those just laws by which he governs the world.

Prayer claims to rest on an absolute trust in God, but does it not rather betray a want of trust? If we believe that he cares for us and is ever seeking our good, ought we not rather to accept our lives as he is shaping them? We can be certain that he is always right, and, in asking him for something he may not have planned, we show doubt of his wisdom and goodness. It was maintained long ago in a dialogue attributed to Plato that a truly pious man will abstain from prayer, for that which in our ignorance we conceive to be best for us is often worst. We pray for it and it is granted to us, and we discover too late that it has been our ruin. The same argument has been put forward many times since, and every one must admit the truth of it:

> We often beg our harms, which the wise powers
> Deny us for our good.

If we believe that God is guiding us ought we not to leave everything in his hands and accept from him without question what he chooses to give?

All such reasoning, however, is based on a false conception of man's relation to God. The trust in God which it contemplates is only fatalism under another name. All things happen inevitably, and our wisdom therefore is to consent to them and never even wish to have them otherwise. This, however, is to put trust in God on the same level as that blind obedience to natural law by which a stone rolls down a hill. We pray for the very reason that we do not belong to the mechanical order. The first man who ever prayed was conscious of two things—that he had a will of his own and that there was another will with which he had to co-operate. God can never have intended that we should submit to him passively, for he has given us personality and the power to think and choose. In prayer we acknowledge the will of

God and yet exercise our own will. You tell God what you desire and seek also to know what he desires. You ask things from him in the confidence that he will grant them if they are not contrary to his wiser purpose. There is therefore nothing presumptuous in prayer, for since God has endowed us with a nature similar, in a smaller measure, to his own, he will allow us to speak to him and will take our human wishes into account. He will deal with us as rational beings. He will not force his desires on us, but will listen to our desires, and grant them if they fit in with his larger plan.

It is in virtue of our personality that we pray, and prayer, in its essence, is individual, springing, as it does, from the knowledge that at the core of our being we are separate souls, and belong, not to other men or to this world, but to God alone. What you cannot confide even to your nearest friend you can tell, without any reserve, to God. You know that to him your inmost life is open and that you can seek help from him in troubles which no one else can share with you or understand. Yet in all times men have joined together to pray, so much so that human society has grown out of common prayer. An ancient tribe or city became conscious of its unity through the festivals at which all assembled and offered the stated prayers. In our modern world we still gather instinctively to pray under stress of any crisis or disaster, and as we thus pray together we feel that we are one and can confront the peril with a single heart. How is it that our most personal act is also that which brings us closest to our fellow-men? It does so for the very reason that it is personal. In the presence of God each one discloses his inner self, and while he prays in company with the others he finds that their heartfelt desires are the same as his own. It is through common prayer that we come to understand each other. We are separate persons but beneath our differences we have the same ultimate needs and the same trust in God. We draw nearest to him in our own souls when we unite in prayer with our brethren.

Jesus speaks in a large number of his sayings of the nature and purpose of prayer, and of the manner in which it should be offered. It is evident that he had meditated deeply on this subject. He was alive to all that was true and beautiful in earlier prayers, but saw that in large measure they had missed their aim. The prayer he taught his disciples is the final outcome of all his thinking on this central act of worship. He summed up in a concrete example his whole conception of what a prayer should be, how it should be framed, what petitions should be made in it, what should be our attitude of mind when we approach God in prayer. There have been many expositions of the Lord's Prayer, but we are thrown back in the end on that which Jesus himself has given us in his various sayings. All that they teach us is illustrated in his prayer.

He declares repeatedly that the object of prayer is to ask God for what we need. We are utterly dependent on God, and we cannot hope to receive from him unless we ask. At times, however, he would seem to indicate that such prayer is unnecessary. Our heavenly Father knows what we need before we ask him. It is his nature to give freely and he sends the rain and the sunshine on all alike. He feeds the sparrows and much more will provide for us, his children. In some of the sayings the idea of asking is set aside altogether and prayer is regarded simply as the means of knowing God and keeping ourselves in harmony with his will. Prayer is answered whenever it enables us to act as God desires. So the writer of Hebrews can truly say that when Jesus prayed with strong crying and tears to him who was able to save him from death, his prayer was heard. He learned what God required of him, and this was the answer he had sought.

Yet for Jesus, as for those before him, prayer consisted in asking. God indeed knows our wants and supplies them ungrudgingly, but he only bestows his gifts when we pray for them. "Ask and ye shall receive; seek and ye shall find; knock and it shall be opened unto you." This demand may seem to be inconsistent with the other idea of the free generosity of God, but it rests on a profound principle which is involved in the very nature of things. Nothing is ever obtained without asking. God provides food for the sparrows, but only when they seek it. The products of the earth are waiting for man's use, but it is for him to find them out and make them his own. He has access to all the treasures of love and wisdom but he must first desire them and so act that they will come to him. Entrance is always free, but you must knock at every gate before it opens. Jesus applies this rule to our whole relation to God, who is willing to give us everything but on the one condition that we ask. In his own ministry he always insisted that those whom he wished to help should themselves take the first step. The sick had to ask for healing. The sinners had to repent. Would-be disciples had to give up their possessions and follow him. He tested men's faith by the effort they made in face of difficulties, and sometimes he put hindrances in their way in order to discover whether they had faith to overcome them. He believed that God acts in the same manner. He has gifts to bestow and is anxious to bestow them, but he will not do so without our seeking. Whatever we need from him we must ask in prayer.

For Jesus, therefore, prayer is a form of action. He has nothing but scorn for prayers which are no more than words, however eloquent and reverential. Prayer cannot be real unless it is conjoined with the endeavour to act by the will of God. On this ground it has been held that Paul's doctrine of justification by faith is in conflict with the teaching of Jesus. He denies all value to works, while Jesus lays the whole stress on what you actually do. But there is no contradiction. Jesus calls for trust in God, and makes everything depend on it. But he requires that it should be genuine, and it cannot be so unless it manifests itself in deeds. Paul also thinks of faith as an energy which creates in us a new life. It is the spring of action, and if no action results from it it is not true faith.

Prayer, therefore, as Jesus conceives of it is that act of ours which enables God to act on our behalf. He will do nothing unless we ask him. That simple act of ours will set his power in motion, as a great ship may be launched by the touch of a child's finger. But the prayer must be a real one, and Jesus has much to say of the conditions which make it real. It is necessary, first of all, to wait on God with a true conception of his nature. Unless you know whom you are addressing you cannot rightly speak to him. So it was the chief aim of Jesus' teaching to change our attitude to God, and by doing this he gave a new meaning to prayer. Hitherto God had been only the great Sovereign, whom men might approach from a distance, with dread and self-abasement. He was placed so high above his creation that he could himself take no knowledge of it, and ruled through a host of angels, who acted as his intermediaries. For Jesus God was the Father, who is near to men and knows them one by one. Prayer was no longer an act of homage to the invisible King but a personal fellowship with God, as of a son with his father. Yet while he was so near to men he was the eternal God, and they must never forget that he was far above them. Their attitude in prayer must be one of love and also of boundless reverence.

Again Jesus bids us pray with an unquestioning faith. We must believe that God hears us, and that whatever we ask for we shall receive. If the prayer seems to be rejected we must go on repeating it, certain that it will be answered in the end. Even when we ask for something that is utterly beyond our reach we must dare to pray for it, confident that with God all things are possible. Jesus is aware that men are incapable of such trust in God, and reflects sadly that when the Son of man returns, at the very end of time, he will not find faith on earth. To this lack of faith he attributes the apparent failure of so many prayers. We ask for gifts that are not granted us, but the reason is that we have never in our hearts expected them. "If ye had faith as a grain of mustard-seed ye should say to this mountain, Be removed and cast into the sea, and it would be done for you." This is spoken figuratively, and Jesus never desired that we should ask for anything that is plainly contrary to the laws of nature. This, to his mind, would not be prayer but an impious tempting of God. Yet in one sense his words may be taken literally. He believed that prayer was an irresistible power. Men keep wondering whether it ever accomplishes anything, but they are doubtful of it because they have never really prayed. If they could only wait on God with an absolute faith they would find that there is no possible limit to the power of prayer.

Faith cannot exist without sincerity, and it is on this aspect of prayer that Jesus most often dwells, for it is within our own control. The best of men, with all their efforts, are weak in faith, but every one can at least be honest in his approach to God. He can state in plain terms what he really wants, not asking for one thing while he secretly desires the opposite. In their intercourse with one another men have constantly to disguise their thoughts and motives, and they foolishly

try to do this in the presence of God, who knows them altogether. They assume a show of piety which corresponds to
nothing real. They pretend to high aspirations of which there
is no evidence in their actual lives. Jesus perceived that it
was this hypocrisy, more than anything else, which made
most prayers ineffectual. It is not to our words that God
listens but to our desires and purposes. The Pharisees while
they prayed were seeking for the applause of men and it
was granted them, for in this motive they were sincere.
"Verily I say to you, they have their reward." They would
need to seek the higher things with an equal sincerity before
God heeded their prayers.

There was another condition of prayer which Jesus deemed
of primary importance. Again and again he takes occasion
to mention it, and he makes a place for it among the petitions of the Lord's Prayer. If God is to hear us we must put
ourselves right with our fellow-men. "When you remember at
the altar that your brother has something against you, first be
reconciled with your brother and then come and offer your
gift." "If you forgive not men their trespasses neither will
God forgive your trespasses." It is not merely that God will
deal with us as we have dealt with others, for it would go
hard with every man if this measure were strictly applied,
and no one could ever dare to pray. The meaning plainly
is that selfishness creates a barrier between ourselves and
God. So long as we feel bitterly towards other men we are
out of harmony with God, who is generous and forgiving.
We have nothing in common with him, and cannot draw
near to him in prayer. It is often assumed that the real interest of Jesus was in human relations, and that his religion
was only a background to his moral and social teaching. But
the truth, when we look deeper, was the other way. His first
concern was with our relation to God. He thought of our

dealings with other men only as the means whereby we could serve God and have more of his nature in ourselves. According as we show mercy to those around us we grow in sympathy with God, and can hold fellowship with him in prayer.

Again, he impresses on us that before we can rightly pray we must be at peace not only with our fellow-men but with ourselves. Our life is passed in a constant turmoil, and amidst all the distractions we do not know what we should pray for. We are beset with present difficulties and are anxious about the future. Our motives and desires are all in conflict, and our prayers defeat themselves as we ask for one thing and all the time are wanting another. Jesus tells us that we must have inward tranquillity before we can rightly pray. He tells us also how it may be obtained. We must lift ourselves above this world and all its vexations and set our minds on God's great purpose. "Seek ye first the Kingdom of God, and all these things shall be added unto you." This, for Jesus, must be the guiding motive in prayer. We have many things to ask for, and we grow bewildered as they crowd in upon our minds. But everything is included in the one desire that God's will should be done on earth. When we are intent on the end towards which we are travelling the difficulties of the journey will right themselves as we go along. We can be confident that everything we need will be granted us if it accords with God's own purpose.

Jesus not only speaks generally of the nature of prayer but gives specific directions as to how we should pray. Sometimes it might appear as if he wished to do away with every kind of formality. Judaism in his day had become ceremonial, and elaborate rules were laid down for the performance of all acts of worship. The least departure from these rules was supposed to vitiate the whole act. Jesus declares, again and again, that the forms matter nothing, and that they only tend to make the action a mechanical one, which could have no value with God. The publican who could do nothing but strike his breast in contrition had offered a true prayer, while the eloquent Pharisee was not heard. Yet it is evident that Jesus saw the necessity of common prayer, which is not possible without stated forms. He took part himself in the prayers of the synagogue. He venerated the Temple as the house of prayer, where the nation met to worship according to the age-long ordinances. If he condemned ritual it was only because it so easily becomes a substitute for heart-felt reverence and desire. Two men went up to the Temple to pray. They were both joining in a formal worship, but to one it was only a form while the other made it a real communion with God.

For Jesus, therefore, prayer must always be personal, even when it is offered in set terms by a company worshipping together. He tells us how we should pray if our act is to have this personal quality. The ideal prayer, he says, is that which is uttered in solitude, in an inner chamber, with the doors barred. All distractions, all thoughts of onlookers are thus excluded. You can feel that you are alone with God and that nothing exists for you but God and your own soul. But it is not the external conditions which make this solitude. When you are in utter privacy you can be drawn aside by your own thoughts just as much as in a crowd, and perhaps more so. The true inner chamber is that which you make for yourself, wherever you happen to pray. You must feel that you personally are in the presence of God.

To make this individual approach you need first of all to forget the world around you. In the time of Jesus a man's reputation depended on his piety, and to a great extent it is so still. There is always a presumption, and surely a well-founded one, that a religious man is trustworthy, that he acts by higher motives and has larger interests than other men. It is often hard to judge how far he lives up to his profession. None of us is quite sure of that himself. When we show ourselves to be religious how far are we thinking of our own credit, of our attachment to some class or party, of the example we ought to show to others? We need constantly to ask ourselves whether our religion holds when nobody is looking at us. This is the test of its reality, and Jesus has this in mind when he bids us pray in secret. Although he is ever rebuking hypocrites he here enjoins on us a noble hypocrisy. When you fast, he says, you are to look your brightest, so that no one will be aware of it. When you pray you are to withdraw yourself from the sight of men, and they will never regard you as a religious man. You are thus to safeguard yourself from every temptation to mix up your worldly interests with your service of God.

But prayer should be made in secret because its very object is to get direction from God. In our ordinary decisions we have to take many things into account; what will be most profitable, what will please our friends and family, what will best fit in with the conditions under which we live. As a rule we follow the course which answers to these requirements, although it may not bé ideally the best. But in prayer we deliberately ask God's judgment, and if we are to have it all disturbing influences must be shut out. We cannot hear the voice of God if it is drowned in the babble of all the other voices. So in prayer we must be alone with God. When a man is only one in a crowd he does not feel his own responsibility. He does not even know his own mind, for he cannot but move with the others. If God is to direct us we must listen to him in secret.

In view of these requirements Jesus lays down certain rules which are to guide us in offering prayer. He demands, for one thing, that it should be expressed in simple language. The idea had grown up that the more elaborate a prayer was made the more it would be acceptable to God. As a result prayers were often little more than accumulations of high-sounding words. Men were impressed by them, and this, as Jesus perceived, was apt to be the chief intention of those who made them. They were not really addressed to God but only to the by-standers, who would admire the flow of language and the piety which must have inspired it. Jesus declared that true prayer would inevitably be simple. In speaking to God, who already knew what was in his heart, a man would feel no need to explain and amplify. He would tell what he desired in the plainest words.

A prayer should likewise be brief. We indeed have countless needs, and might go on forever recounting them, but only a few of them are essential, and we must learn to distinguish these from the others. This is one of the chief purposes of prayer. As we wait in the presence of God we see things in their true proportion, and think of our fundamental needs. The more we realise them the more we shall express them in the fewest words. Jesus says of the scribes and Pharisees that for a pretence they make long prayers and will receive greater condemnation (Matt. 23:14). The idea is partly that they offer words instead of actions, but it is also implied that they were occupied with things that mattered little. They had no burning desires; they had never understood what they needed from God, and wearied him with trifling questions which they might have answered for themselves. We must speak to God of what we most require of him, and if we are in earnest there will be no waste of words. Jesus bade us be utterly straightforward in our intercourse with other men. "Let your yea be yea and your nay nay, for whatever is more than this is vanity." The same rule applies, and far more emphatically, to our converse with God.

But while prayer should be brief and concise it must also be insistent. In several of his parables Jesus dwells on this theme of importunity in prayer. He tells how a widow won her plea because she never ceased repeating it until she was listened to; how a man opened his door at last because the knocking went on continually. In like manner men must keep praying and never despair. It is not that God is unwilling to answer us, but he desires that we should come to him with a will so determined that it cannot miss its purpose. This, for Jesus, is the necessary element in prayer. You must mean what you say. You must not lose confidence in God even when he seems to deny your petition. Prayer has no value if it does not arise from this trust in God, and if the trust is genuine it will be persistent. If you give up after the first discouragement there is no trust, and therefore no true prayer.

Besides the many sayings on the nature of prayer we have examples in the Gospels of Jesus' own prayers, from the beginning of his ministry to his last moments on the Cross. They are all in keeping with the directions he gives in his teaching. His recorded prayers are brief and simple and direct. They are reverent and spring from a sense of intimacy. Their aim is to obtain the help of God in urgent difficulties but behind them is always a calm faith in God, even though his help should be withheld. The greatest prayer ever uttered was that of Jesus in Gethsemane. Perhaps it is this one rather than the other which ought to be called preeminently the Lord's Prayer. It breathes an intense certainty of the nearness and the power and the goodness of God. It is a cry for help in a desperate moment, when only the hand of God could be of any avail. Yet the desire at the heart of it is for inward strength to submit to God, whatever he might choose to give. "Not my will but thine be done."

To understand the prayer he taught his disciples we must consider it in the light of his various sayings and of his own attitude when he prayed. His object when he made the prayer was to sum up, once for all, his whole conception of what prayer should be, and this is how men have regarded it in all times since. They have treasured it not only for its own sake but as the pattern to which all prayer should conform. How ought we to pray? This is the primary question in religion, for religion, in the last resort, consists in prayer. The question has been answered for us by him who best knew the mind of God. "After this manner pray ye."

CHAPTER II

THE RECORDS OF THE PRAYER

Two of the evangelists, Matthew and Luke, have recorded the Lord's Prayer, and at a number of points they are at variance. In substance they are in full agreement, but Luke makes several omissions, and sometimes changes a word employed by Matthew. It needs to be remembered that they both translate the prayer from the language spoken by Jesus, but this does not explain all the variations. There must have been two different versions of what Jesus had said, and we cannot but ask ourselves which was the more authentic.

Before considering this question we have to consider another difference between the two evangelists. They seem to disagree as to the circumstances in which the prayer was given. Matthew places it in the Sermon on the Mount, as part of a discourse in which Jesus, at the beginning of his ministry, set forth the main elements of his new message. Among other things he spoke of prayer and impressed on his hearers that it should be sincere and personal, framed in simple language, uttering directly what was in their hearts. Then he gave them this prayer to illustrate what he meant. It can be proved, however, that the Sermon on the Mount is for the most part a collection of Jesus' sayings, put together by Matthew himself. Jesus may indeed have begun his public work by some kind of manifesto, declaring what he had set himself to teach, and showing how he differed from teachers before him. Luke in his 6th chapter also reports a discourse which is similar in the main to the Sermon on the Mount, though much shorter. But Matthew has used this briefer statement as a nucleus around which he has gathered a great number of Jesus' primary sayings, spoken on various occasions during the whole course of his ministry. The object is to present the new teaching in a compendious form, so that the reader may know at the outset what to look for in the history that follows. One of those additional utterances which have been brought into the Sermon on the Mount is the Lord's Prayer.

Matthew's account of how it was first delivered cannot, therefore, be taken literally. He is no doubt right in his principal idea that Jesus wished to illustrate the nature of true prayer. He may be right, also, in assigning the prayer to a period near the beginning of the ministry. But we cannot accept his view of the occasion on which it was given or of the context in which Jesus spoke it. Matthew has recognised the outstanding value of the prayer, and has therefore made a place for it in his collection of the primary sayings. But all that we learn from him is that after he had gathered around him a company of followers Jesus taught them to pray in these words.

Luke is much more specific. He tells us (Luke 11:1–4) that the disciples were once present with Jesus while he prayed, and when he had finished one of them said, "Lord, teach us to pray, as John also taught his disciples." By way of answer Jesus gave them the Lord's Prayer. We are not told when or where the incident took place, but Luke apparently thinks of it as happening well on in the ministry, when Jesus had won a large following, comparable to that of John the Baptist. This would seem to be the reason why the disciples made their request. They were not asking how to frame a prayer, for they were deeply religious men, who had been praying all their lives. They wanted a distinctive prayer which might be used by their community now that it had a place of its own and was growing in importance. It was the custom of prominent teachers in that day to compose special prayers for the society they had formed. A number of the prayers now adopted into the Jewish liturgy had their origin in this manner, and John had followed the usual practice. His prayer would doubtless express his conviction that the Kingdom of God was at hand and that men must repent and live righteously in view of the approaching Judgment. Jesus' disciples wanted a prayer which would represent their own Master's teaching. They asked for it, we are told, after they had heard him praying and the difference between his thought and that of John had impressed itself on their minds.

Due weight must be given to this account in Luke, which may preserve a good tradition that Jesus made his prayer at the special request of his disciples. It is quite possible, too, that there was some connection between his prayer and that which had been taught by John. Jesus, we know, thought reverently of his predecessor, and probably took over from him much more than can now be ascertained. At the time when Luke wrote, the community founded by John was still flourishing, and there are clear indications both in Luke's Gospel and in his book of Acts that he was well acquainted with it. He must often have heard John's prayer and marked its correspondence at some points with that of Jesus. But his account may have grown out of his own inferences as he compared the two prayers. He saw in the Lord's Prayer the outcome of some kind of rivalry, not between the two teachers but between their bands of disciples. Those who followed Jesus were proud of their Master, and wished him to do what John had done. Would not he also make a prayer for them, which would resemble that of John and would yet be different and far better? If this was the view of Luke it cannot be accepted. There is no trace of anything like party spirit in the Lord's Prayer. It stands out from all other prayers by its universality. Its whole object is to give utterance to the needs and aspirations of all men, and Jesus cannot have been thinking when he made it of how he differed from some other teacher.

It must be concluded, then, that neither Luke nor Matthew knew anything of the precise occasion when the prayer was given, and perhaps they could not have told from what source they had derived it. For their knowledge of Jesus' teaching they were dependent on a large collection of his sayings, which had been compiled from a number of shorter ones. It never, apparently, took the form of a regular book, and could be added to from time to time as new material came in. Copies that varied widely were thus in circulation, and Matthew made use of one of them, Luke of another, while Mark had access to another, much shorter. But our two accounts of the Lord's Prayer do not seem to be taken from any written source. While other sayings had been put into writing, lest they might be forgotten, no need for this would be felt in the case of the Lord's Prayer. All believers knew it by heart and were constantly repeating it. It was bound up with the very existence of the new religion.

Even if the prayer had come to be included in some

written document it does not follow that the evangelists would take it from that source. They would naturally fall back on that form of it which they were themselves accustomed to use. This might differ from that which they found in writing, but for them it was the Lord's Prayer, hallowed by the practice of a life-time, and they could not bring themselves to change it. Two generations had passed since it was first given, and since then it had been translated into another language and had suffered friction, like a coin which has passed countless times from hand to hand. While it remained substantially the same it was current in each section of the church in slightly different forms, and Matthew belonged to one community and Luke to another. Each of them has recorded the prayer as it was familiar to him in the worship of his own church.

It might seem surprising that in spite of everything the prayer did not remain fixed, in the form given to it by Jesus. All Christians revered it as his, and one might think that the least departure from the consecrated words would at once have been detected and condemned. But it is always the best-known utterances which are most liable to be altered in common use. Every one makes them his own, and adapts them unconsciously to his own purpose. Familiar lines of Shakspeare are seldom quoted correctly. The hymn most often sung is "Rock of Ages," but there are no two hymn-books which agree on the exact words, and all the versions are different from the author's own. We have to allow for this process of modification in the Lord's Prayer. Each company that prayed it was led to vary the words, so as to convey new needs by means of it, and this was in full accord with Jesus' own intention. He did not wish that the prayer should be said mechanically, as if there were some magical virtue in the words themselves. He meant that our own

minds should be active, that his prayer should also be ours.
It contained the substance of what we should pray for, and
he left us free to change the form. This was fully understood
in the early church.

The two accounts, then, differ from each other, much
more than might appear from the ordinary text of the New
Testament. Here we have to reckon with a difficulty which
meets us constantly in the study of the Gospels. They are
similar works made largely out of the same materials, but
they are also different and sometimes contradict each other.
The early copyists were always under the temptation to
bring them into agreement. It was assumed that when two
evangelists varied in their report of the same event or saying this was due to some oversight or accident, which it was
the duty of a good scribe to correct. This feeling was particularly strong in the case of the Lord's Prayer. All Christians were required to join in the prayer, and yet there were
two accounts of it which both had Gospel authority. Luke's
version, therefore, was assimilated to that of Matthew, and
only the most ancient manuscripts have preserved his text
in something like its original form. Even these have to be
carefully checked against each other, for copyists had been
anxious, almost from the beginning, to make the two versions agree.

When the manuscript evidence has been sifted it would
appear that the prayer as recorded in Luke was in these
terms: "Father, thy name be hallowed; Let thy Kingdom
come; Give us day by day our daily bread; And forgive us
our sins, for we also forgive every man who owes us; And
bring us not into temptation." The prayer is essentially the
same as in Matthew, but a number of differences are at
once apparent.

Looking first at the prayer as a whole, Luke's version is shorter than Matthew's, and is more individual in character. In Matthew a community is supposed to be worshipping together, and the prayer is composed in rhythmical language, so that all may join their voices as in a hymn. Luke also thinks of the prayer as communal. It is he who tells us that Jesus gave it to his disciples in answer to their request for such a prayer. This idea is so far preserved that every petition is for "us" and not for "me." But the emphasis is clearly on the personal needs of those who offer the common prayer, while in Matthew we are never allowed to forget that a community is praying. At an early time an addition was made to Matthew's version in order to bring out quite explicitly its communal purpose. "For thine is the Kingdom and the power and the glory." These words do not belong to the original prayer. They are not found in any early manuscript and have their counterpart in liturgical prayers of the time. Their object is plainly liturgical. The Lord's Prayer, in Matthew's version of it, was meant for a community, and the church fitted it with the closing ascription which was customary in common prayer.

When we turn from the prayer as a whole to its separate parts the differences between the two versions are these. At the opening, Luke has the single word "Father" instead of "Our Father in heaven." The petition "Thy will be done on earth as it is in heaven" is omitted altogether. "Give us to-day" becomes general, "Give us day by day." "Our debts" is changed into "our trespasses," but here there is no real difference, for the Aramaic word for "sins" was "debts," and this idiom is preserved by Luke in the second part of the petition, "as we forgive our debtors." Here, however, the present tense is used; "we forgive," instead of "we have forgiven," as in Matthew. Finally, the last petition "Deliver us from evil" is left out.

In the view of some scholars another difference, more remarkable than any of these, should be added. It is known that in Marcion's edition of Luke's Gospel, about the middle of the second century, "Thy Kingdom come" appeared in this form: "May thy holy Spirit come upon us and cleanse us." Marcion was a heretic, and it has commonly been assumed that he deliberately changed the words of the prayer to suit his own teaching. But there is good evidence that he took over a variation of the prayer which was already current, and which was approved by some of the early Fathers. It is noteworthy that in the same chapter which contains the Lord's Prayer Luke records the saying, "If ye therefore give good gifts unto your children will not your heavenly Father give the holy Spirit to those who ask him?" May there not be a reference here to something he had just said in the prayer? It has therefore been held that Marcion was faithful to the original text and that it was changed at a later time to bring Luke's version into harmony with that of Matthew. For many reasons this is difficult to believe. The petition "Thy Kingdom come" is the central one of the prayer, and Luke could not possibly have replaced it with another. Moreover, the idea of the cleansing power of the Spirit was one that grew up in the later church. There is no trace of it in Jesus' own teaching, and it cannot have had a place in any primitive account of the prayer. It is evident, too, that Luke thinks of the prayer as concerned with the elementary needs of life, and he cannot have gone out of his way to bring in a theological doctrine. The variation which crept into his text may be simply explained from that saying in the passage which follows. Jesus there declares that God will give the Spirit to those who ask him. This suggested that a petition for the Spirit should accompany the prayer, and Paul's idea of the cleansing power of the Spirit was added.

This other petition came to be substituted by some worshippers for the original one, "Thy Kingdom come."

The two versions of the prayer thus differ, at important points, from one another, and the question at once arises which is the more authentic. Many scholars have given the preference to that of Luke. It is the shorter of the two, and the aim of Jesus was to show that genuine prayer should be brief and simple. Again, it is free from all formality. It begins with the one word "Father," and the language throughout is quite unstudied, with no attempt at rhythmical structure. This perfect naturalness, it is claimed, is what we should expect from Jesus. Again, it is made up wholly of petitions, directly stated, while in Matthew the petitions have explanations added to them: "Our Father," that is our heavenly one; "Thy Kingdom," that is the coming time when thy will is done; "lead us not into temptation," due to a power of evil from which we need to be delivered. All this seems to suggest later reflection on the thought of Jesus, while Luke confines himself to what he actually said.

It cannot be assumed, however, that the shorter version must for that reason be the more original. A statement of any kind is just as often shortened as lengthened in the course of transmission, indeed much more often. The very fact that Jesus had required prayer to be brief would induce many of his followers to leave out from his own prayer everything that might appear superfluous. The truth is that in the prayer as Matthew gives it there is not a word too much. Addressing God as Father we must yet wait on him reverently, knowing that he is high above this world. Looking for his Kingdom in the future we must never forget that even now his will is active and supreme. Praying that we may not fall into temptation we should ask deliverance from evil into which we have already fallen. The more closely we examine the prayer the more we find that there is nothing that can be left out. Neither is there anything that is merely formal. The language may not be that of common speech, but in the act of prayer we do not speak familiarly as to our fellow-men. We are conscious of the majesty of God and this sense of awe reflects itself in the words we use. It comes as a shock to every one when terms of daily business are intruded into a prayer.

The modern criticism of the Gospels has become obsessed with the idea that the teaching of Jesus was moulded into its present form by the later church. It is assumed that he talked freely with his disciples, who remembered the substance of what he said; but as time went on the thoughts he had expressed in everyday language were crystallised in beautiful and incisive words. There is every evidence, however, that he possessed in a very high degree the poetic gift of utterance. The people heard him gladly, as they would never have done if his speech had been dull and boring. His sayings fixed themselves in the memory, not only because they dealt with great truths, but because they conveyed these truths in language that fitted them perfectly. So if Luke's version of the Lord's Prayer is only a bare summary of what we find in Matthew, this is no proof that it is more authentic. On the contrary, it lacks the surest mark by which we recognise the utterance of Jesus. Particularly when he made his prayer he was anxious to give of his very best. There can be no greater mistake than to conceive of the prayer as thrown out casually, in any words that happened to offer themselves at the moment. It was certainly the outcome of meditation, and every word has been fully considered, and put in its right place. Jesus was seeking to make a prayer which would sum up all he had been teaching, and which would be constantly repeated by his followers and treasured by them as a lasting possession. That version of the prayer which bears the clearest marks of careful study in its structure and language is most likely to come nearest to what he said.

There are several more definite reasons for accepting the record in Matthew. For one thing, it is Hebraic in character, and is largely based, as we shall see, on the prayers commonly used in the synagogue. This would be natural to Jesus, who lived in Palestine and thought and spoke in the manner of his country. Very shortly after his death the church broke away from Judaism, and sought to present the Christian message in forms more intelligible to the Gentile world. The prayer as Luke gives it seems to reflect this later effort to divest the new ideas of their Jewish associations, and to this extent it is not the prayer as Jesus himself spoke it. Again, Luke omits two petitions which we find in Matthew, and these, when we examine them, are organic to the prayer. It does not properly hold together without them, and their omission must be due to a misunderstanding. They are retained in Matthew's version because it gives the prayer in its original form. In this connection the change of "debts" into "trespasses" is highly significant. An Aramaic word is replaced, in Luke's version, by one which makes its meaning more intelligible, but the petition goes on "as we forgive our debtors." The whole sentence must have stood originally as Matthew gives it. It may be added that in Matthew the prayer is clearly one in which a community may join. Luke himself tells us that this was its purpose, but there is nothing in his version, apart from the use of the plural number, that suggests a company of people praying in unison. Since this was Jesus' intention it may be inferred that Matthew has preserved the prayer as he had made it.

One further evidence tells strongly on the side of Matthew. Besides the two versions in the Gospels we have another of very early date,—that which is contained in the Didachê, the short manual of church order which was drawn up, most probably, about the middle of the second century. It enjoins on all Christians that they should pray three times a day as the Lord commanded in his Gospel, that is, in his own acknowledged teaching. Then it recites the Lord's Prayer, almost exactly as it is found in Matthew. There is only one difference of any importance, the substitution of "our debt" for "our debts,"—not our daily offences against God but the evil inherent in our sinful nature. The closing Doxology also, which does not appear in the best manuscripts of Matthew, is appended in the form "for thine is the power and the glory." It would thus appear that the author does not merely copy from Matthew but gives the prayer as it was generally used in the church of his day. It had come down in unbroken tradition from the Lord himself, and this was the form in which it must be repeated. The evidence of the Didachê is of secondary value, but we can at least gather from it that there was one version of the prayer on which the early church was generally in agreement, and it was that which Matthew has put on record. He gives the words of Jesus as nearly as they could be remembered by those who heard them first.

The prayer is recorded, then, with some variations but substantially in the same way, by two of the evangelists, but why not by the others? Mark wrote the earliest Gospel, and if he had given his version it might have been decisive, but he never mentions the prayer, and this has often been regarded as one of the riddles of the New Testament. To be sure he is concerned with the acts of Jesus rather than his words, but in a number of places he tells us something of the teaching, and why does he omit this central part of it? The prayer, indeed, might well have been included among Jesus' actions, for by means of it he had laid down an ordinance which his people were to observe whenever they met together. A record of his ministry which said nothing of his prayer might seem to lack one of its essential elements. The inference has sometimes been drawn that Mark leaves out the prayer because it was no true part of the history. It had grown up somehow out of later Christian worship and was ascribed to Jesus, but this first historian, confining himself to the known facts, could say nothing of it.

This cannot, however, explain its absence from the Fourth Gospel, which was written considerably later than the others. The author cannot possibly have been ignorant of the prayer. He was acquainted with the Gospels in which it was recorded. The repetition of it was a regular part of the service of the church and of the private devotions of every loyal Christian. And this, perhaps, is the reason why it is not recorded either by Mark or John. It was the one element of Jesus' teaching which could be taken for granted. All Christians knew it by heart and the writer of a Gospel might well think to himself that there was no need to put it formally on record. The author of the Epistle to the Hebrews tells his readers that he will pass on to higher instruction, "leaving aside the rudiments of the teaching of Christ" (Heb. 6:1). It is no doubt on this principle that the New Testament never tells us why the church adopted the rite of baptism or held its meetings on the first day of the week. These were fundamental ordinances which had simply to be accepted, and it was the same with the Lord's Prayer. Mark is not primarily concerned with Jesus' teaching, and leaves out a great deal of what he must have known. He would feel that, if there was anything he could omit, it was the prayer with which every one was familiar. It was in no danger of being forgotten and did not need to be safeguarded in a book.

John may have had further reasons for omitting it. He thinks of Christ as the divine Word, one in nature with the Father, and the prayer may have seemed to him out of harmony with this conception. The question has often been raised in later times whether Jesus included himself in the petitions he taught to his disciples. Did he, too, ask forgiveness for his trespasses, and deliverance from evil and temptation? John may have been troubled by such difficulties, and have decided for this reason to omit the prayer. Moreover his mind was mystical, and prayer for him was an inward fellowship with God through Christ. The mystical note appeared to be absent from the prayer. Later teachers tried to read it in, and interpreted the prayer, by allegorical methods, in a purely spiritual sense. John would not thus wrest the words from their obvious meaning, and preferred to leave out the prayer altogether. We cannot doubt that he joined with other Christians in praying it, but he is seeking in his Gospel to present that other side of the work of Christ which it seemed to leave out of sight.

But while the prayer is omitted in Mark and John there are clear traces of it in both these Gospels. Mark tells us how Jesus prayed in Gethsemane, "Abba, Father, not what I will but what thou wilt." In the passage which follows we read how he warned his disciples, "Watch and pray that ye enter not into temptation." We cannot but feel that in his whole description of the Agony Mark has the Lord's Prayer in his mind. It cannot truly be said that he leaves the prayer out of his Gospel, for in this culminating scene he gives us the very substance of it. John does not record the story of the Agony, but in place of it he tells how Jesus, on the eve of his death, was overcome with a terrible anxiety. "Now is my soul troubled, and what shall I say? Father, save me from this hour, but for this cause came I unto this hour. Father, glorify thy name." These last words are almost an exact repetition of the opening words of the Lord's Prayer. It is more than probable, too, that he was thinking of the prayer when he described how Jesus, after the Last Supper, prayed for his disciples and for the community which would arise through their message. The two prayers have little in common, but they both embody the same idea that the people of Christ are bound together by a prayer that came from Christ himself. The great 17th chapter of John is inspired by the Lord's Prayer, and is meant, in some measure, to interpret it.

Outside of the Gospels there is no account of the prayer in the New Testament. This is not surprising, for Paul and the other writers are not occupied, like the evangelists, with the life and teaching of Jesus. They accept the historical facts and are intent on explaining them, in their moral and spiritual significance. Nevertheless we might have expected that the prayer would be mentioned, at least incidentally. It held such a central place in Christian life and worship that the absence of all reference to it may well appear strange. And when we look more closely we can perceive that while these later writers do not speak of it explicitly it was constantly in their minds. They insist on prayer as the one thing needful in the service of Christ, and this could not but suggest to their readers the prayer which he himself had taught. In one sense these teachers are always alluding to the Lord's Prayer. They tell us that we must wait on God with reverence and also with child-like trust, that we must look for his Kingdom and at the same time ask him for all things necessary to this earthly life, that we must desire his forgiveness, his protection, his help in resisting all forms of evil. All the New Testament teaching is in line with the Lord's Prayer and takes the knowledge of it for granted.

Here and there we come on passages which seem to point to it directly. Paul declares in a well-known verse in Romans (8:15) "Ye have received the Spirit of adoption whereby we cry Abba, Father." The statement is amplified in Galatians (4:6) "Because ye are sons God hath sent forth the Spirit of his Son into your hearts, crying Abba, Father." It can hardly be doubted that there is here a reference to the opening of the Lord's Prayer. In the invocation of God as Father Paul sees the new and distinctive thing in the Christian message. It was apparently the custom in Gentile communities to add the Aramaic word for Father to the Greek one. Jesus had prayed in his own language, and the very word he had used was repeated, so as to signify that it was through him men had obtained the privilege of addressing God as "our Father." Paul seems also to have the Lord's Prayer in mind when he says to the Corinthians (I Cor. 10:13) "There hath no temptation taken you but such as is common to men; but God is faithful, who will not suffer you to be tempted beyond your power, but with the temptation will make a way of escape, that ye may be able to bear it." This is perhaps the best interpretation of that petition in the prayer which has always been the most perplexing. God has indeed ordained that all men should be tempted; but as he leads us into temptation he also provides the deliverance, if we only follow his way of escape.

It would not be difficult to collect many passages from Paul's Epistles and from the other New Testament writings which remind us of the Lord's Prayer; but there is little that can be set down to definite allusion. This was inevitable from the nature of the prayer. It sums up in a concentrated form the whole substance of Jesus' teaching. It also reflects his attitude to God and his conception of man's life and destiny. Little distinction can thus be made between the general teaching of Jesus and this particular prayer. There is not a verse in the New Testament which does not have some bearing on Jesus and his message, and to this extent the whole book is like a commentary on his prayer. The value of the prayer consists in this, that it represents the mind of Christ. In all ages men have kept reciting it day by day, in order to remind themselves that they are Christ's servants and must try this day to follow in his steps. The prayer, even when they say it thoughtlessly, is the abiding symbol of their belief in Christ and in his way of life. So it is not surprising that the later writers do not expressly mention the prayer or quote its words. This does not mean that they were unmindful of it. In a real sense they were always thinking of it, and it gives meaning to everything they say. Their one purpose is to confirm our faith in the religion of Jesus, which could not be separated from his prayer.

CHAPTER III

THE BACKGROUND

I T was apparent from the first that the Christian message was radically new. Modern criticism has been largely occupied with tracing the affinities between Christian ideas and those of Judaism, of Greek philosophy, of the Eastern cults which had mingled with Western Paganism in the first century. It has been shown that a great number of influences played their part in the moulding of that religion which we now call Christianity. The impression has thus been created that it was nothing but a compound of beliefs and practices already existing, and that something like it would have come into being even if Jesus had never lived. But we know that when the gospel was first proclaimed every one was startled by its newness. The Jewish leaders had Jesus put to death because his religion was quite contrary to their own. The Christian missionaries were mobbed in Pagan cities because "they had turned the world upside down." No one was in a better position to compare Christianity with all existing religions than the Apostle Paul. He knew everything about Judaism; he had grown up in a city which was a centre of philosophical culture and also of the typical Pagan cults.

Yet his judgment was that "old things have passed away; behold all things have become new."

Jesus was himself conscious of the newness of his message. He contrasted it with that given to "those of old time." He adopted methods which were entirely different from those of the Rabbis and even of his predecessor John the Baptist. He came forward as the herald of the Kingdom of God, the new order in which the present one would be completely changed. With this new age in view he called on men to break with the world, to leave all and follow him. He meant his prayer to be the manifesto of his new message. Every religious community in those days had its special prayer, which marked out where it differed from all others. Jesus also formed his body of followers, and it required a prayer which would be distinctive of what it stood for. We might have expected, therefore, that he would make his prayer as different as possible from any that had hitherto been used. Since his object was to enforce a new type of belief, would he not have made this clear by expressing new ideas in novel and striking language? This has been the practice in almost every sect which has devised its own peculiar prayer. Jesus, however, did not do this. We find when we examine his prayer that it is composed out of old materials. For the most part it simply repeats, in much the same language, what men had always been praying for. They would hardly be conscious as they uttered this prayer of Jesus that they were not making the petitions they had made in the past.

In this there is nothing that need surprise us. The great human needs have ever been the same, and have found expression in words that come instinctively to the lips of all men. As they wait on God they speak to him of the things that lie nearest to their hearts, and these elementary needs must always be in essence the same. The very test of a true prayer is that it might have been offered in any age or country. If it merely reflects some passing mood or the conditions of a given time it is not in any real sense a prayer. God never changes and we must speak to him out of that which is deepest and most abiding in ourselves. This is the nature of the Lord's Prayer. All men can join in it, whatever may be their race or class or circumstances. It has the same meaning now as when it was first offered. And it has this quality because there is nothing in it that men had not always in some manner known and felt.

We have first to consider, therefore, how far Jesus availed himself of prayers which had existed long before him. He has certainly done so, and must have done it intentionally. If he had chosen he could easily have put his thought into language which would have impressed every one with its novelty, but he took words and whole sentences which were already familiar to all who heard him. It has often been argued that he has no real title to the prayer which goes by his name. At the most he only borrowed some fragments of existing prayers and pieced them together in a new combination, with some slight additions. But he employs words which themselves are old in order that men may ponder more deeply on their meaning. They are to feel as they utter them "this is our own prayer; it expresses thoughts and desires of which we have always been obscurely conscious, and now we can understand them." This is the secret of all the greatest art and poetry, that it brings home to us what we have always known. You do not say "this is altogether new" but rather "this is what I have always felt myself, though I never realised it till now." So it was the purpose of Jesus that men should see their own minds reflected in his prayer.

Parallels to it can be found in the literature of all religions, even the most ancient of which we have any knowledge. The sacred writings of Egypt and Babylon contain phrases strangely similar to some of those used by Jesus. There are passages in the Persian Zendavesta and the Indian Vedas which remind us of one sentence or another of the Lord's Prayer. Such resemblances must be set down to pure coincidence. It is impossible that Jesus should have borrowed anything from alien religions which he had never even heard of. He falls back on their thought and sometimes on their very words because he deals with beliefs which are inherent in the very nature of man. In so far as those ancient religions had any influence on him it was indirectly, through the Old Testament. Hebrew thought in its earlier phases owed much to Egypt and Babylon, and in later days to Persia. All that it derived from these sources had long, however, been assimilated, and was now a living part of the Jewish religion. It is equally useless to find parallels to the Lord's Prayer in Greek poets and philosophers, although they have much to say that reminds us of it. One of the noblest of all prayers is the Hymn of Cleanthes, written about 250 B.C., from which Paul quoted the words "For we are also his offspring." But Jesus knew nothing of the wisdom of Greece, nor had it affected the religion into which he was born. The one sacred book which he acknowledged was the Old Testament.

Here, then, we must ultimately look for parallels to his prayer, which contains hardly a word that does not recall some Old Testament utterance. "Doubtless thou art our Father." "O Lord who dwellest in the heavens." "Thy Kingdom is an everlasting Kingdom." "Bless the Lord, ye his angels who do his commandments; bless the Lord, O my soul." It would be possible to rewrite the whole of the Lord's

Prayer in words taken from the Old Testament, and for that part from the one book of Psalms. Between the Psalms and the prayer there is plainly a close connection, and it does not reside merely in similarities of language. One cannot but feel that in his approach to God Jesus shares the spirit of the Psalmists. He echoes, it may be said, not only the words of the Psalms but the music to which they are set.

The Psalms, it must never be forgotten, were the hymns sung in the Temple service to the honour of God, and their primary purpose was to express the wonder and exultation which filled the worshippers while standing in his presence. The Hebrew name for them was the "praises" of God, and the prayers they contain spring almost of their own accord, out of the mood of praise. It was said by one of the Rabbis that a prayer should begin with glorifying God, because the petitioner is like a servant who begs a favour from his master and tries first to win him over by words of compliment. This, it must be admitted, is still a very common idea, though it may not be stated so frankly. What we really want when we pray is the gift at God's disposal, and we expect him to give it more readily if we address him in adoring words. But in true prayer the praise is no device or formality, but is the essential part of the act. We pray to God because we are possessed with the sense of his greatness and goodness, and the prayer is the natural outcome of the praise. There are some of the Psalms in which nothing whatever is asked of God. All thought of his gifts is forgotten in the sense of his wisdom and holiness and sovereignty. The prayer of Jesus is conceived in this spirit of praise.

But while it goes back to the Old Testament it does not connect with it directly. Jesus had been accustomed all his life to prayers offered in the synagogue and in private devotion which were founded on scripture. Its language was often repeated literally, but sometimes with additions or modifications due to the requirements of a later time. Jesus had evidently these Jewish prayers in his mind when he composed this one of his own. It has been held that he did nothing more than select from them, and that his prayer belongs not so much to himself as to the Rabbis who drew up the Jewish liturgy. These men, however, would have been the first to admit that they had done very little themselves. They had only followed in the steps of the Psalmists and Prophets. Their task had been to enable the devout worshipper to pray in words consecrated by scripture. It was not directly but through these prayers of the synagogue that Jesus derived his prayer from the Old Testament.

The Jewish prayers have sometimes been disparaged in order to minimise the debt which Jesus owed to them. There is indeed much in them to which we may take exception. They often adopt Old Testament ideas without insight or discrimination. They are verbose and formal. They are inspired by purely national sentiment. The spiritual and the earthly are strangely mingled in them. But it is useless to deny that they are noble religious utterances. They could not have been otherwise since they are taken for the most part from scripture, and often improve on what they borrow. The men who composed them had a real instinct for what was vital in the Old Testament teaching, and this was recognised by Jesus. In so far as they harmonised with his own thought he took over the Jewish prayers, but he does for them what they had themselves done for the Old Testament. Out of the mixed material they offered he fastens on what was best and so makes the perfect prayer.

He had many Jewish prayers to choose from but confines himself to those used in the synagogue or at stated hours

of devotion, and so were known to everybody. Religious
feeling had attached itself to these prayers, and would thus
respond to this new one which he put in their place. We still
require that prayer should conform to certain models, made
sacred by association, and Jesus purposely framed his prayer
in the accepted language of worship. In the synagogue service there were three prayers which were solemnly recited
at every meeting—the *Shema*, the *Kaddish*, and the Eighteen
Benedictions (*Shemone Esreh*). The *Shema* was not so much
a prayer as a confession of faith: "Hear, O Israel, the Lord
thy God is one Lord." This belief in the unity of God was
the cornerstone of the religion of Israel, and the great verse
in Deuteronomy (6:4), with the addition of several others
expressing the same idea, was pronounced at the beginning
of every service. It has no place in the Lord's Prayer but is
presupposed. Men are to pray to God in the sure conviction that there is no other beside him.

The *Kaddish* also was not in the strict sense a prayer. Its
purpose was to ensure that those who prayed should wait
on God in a mood of reverence. Before they asked anything
of him they were to realise who he was, and what was his
will with men. The *Kaddish* consisted of two parts, the first
one preliminary to the service as a whole.

> May his great name be magnified and hallowed in the
> world, which he has made according to his will, and
> may his kingly rule be established in your life-time—
> in your time and in the time of the whole house of
> Israel. May the name of the Lord be praised from now
> on and forever. May the prayer and petition of all
> Israel find acceptance before our Father who is in
> heaven.

The second part of the *Kaddish* preceded the address, delivered by some Rabbi who was present.

Upon Israel and the Rabbis and their scholars and those who learn from their scholars and all who study the Law in this place and everywhere, may there be grace and mercy and compassion and deliverance from our Father who is in heaven.

The affiinities with the Lord's Prayer are at once apparent. God is "our Father in heaven," his Kingdom is coming, his name is hallowed, he is the giver of life and sustenance and deliverance. One similarity is significant. The hallowing of God's name is followed immediately by the prayer for his Kingdom, just as in the Lord's Prayer. This agreement can hardly be accidental. It suggests that the two ideas were connected in the mind of Jesus because they were already connected in the prayer he knew.

The outstanding Jewish prayer was the *Shemone Esreh* or Eighteen Benedictions. It was recited by the congregation at every service in the synagogue, and all pious men were supposed to say it individually three times a day. Owing to its length, permission was given to use two or three of the petitions instead of all the eighteen, and various abridgments, sanctioned by the Rabbis, were also current: for instance, "Grant us knowledge, accept our repentance, forgive us, O our Redeemer, heal our diseases, bless our years." Wise teachers, indeed, insisted that prayers should not be said hurriedly by rote, but that the mind should accompany the words, and that phrases might be added or omitted, and alterations made from time to time. The standard prayer has thus come down to us in several forms, and there can be no doubt that the latter part of it dates from a period subsequent to that of Jesus. The earlier part, however, is certainly ancient. It grew up most probably, like the Psalms, out of the Temple worship, and so passed into general use.

Jesus must have known it from his childhood, and when he made his own prayer it was this one above all others which served him as his model. It will be well to have before us at least the earlier of the eighteen petitions, those which were admittedly used in Jesus' lifetime, and which find echoes in his prayer.

(1) Blessed be thou, O Lord, our God and God of our fathers; God of Abraham, Isaac and Jacob, a mighty and faithful God, a most high God, Creator of heaven and earth, our shield and shield of our fathers, our confidence in all generations. Blessed be thou, O Lord, the shield of Abraham.

(2) Thou art a mighty one who humbles the strong and judges the mighty, the ever-living God who raises the dead, who causes the wind to blow and the dew to fall, who cherishes the living and makes the dead to live. Blessed be thou, O Lord, who quickenest the dead.

(3) Holy and fearful is thy name and there is no God beside thee. Blessed be thou, O Lord, the holy God.

(4) Bestow on us, our Father, knowledge of thee and insight and understanding out of thy Law. Blessed be thou, O Lord, who givest knowledge.

(5) Bring us back to thee, O Lord, that we may return in repentance. Blessed be thou, O Lord, who has pleasure in repentance.

(6) Forgive us, our Father, for we have sinned against thee; blot out our transgressions from before thine eyes, for great is thy mercy. Blessed be thou, O Lord, who forgivest much.

(7) Look on our misery and prosper our cause, and

deliver us for thy name's sake. Blessed be thou, O Lord, deliverer of Israel.

Petitions follow for a bountiful harvest, for the gathering in of the Dispersion, for the re-establishment of the nation. The concluding petitions are strictly national in character, and plainly belong to a period long after Jesus. God is besought to rebuild Jerusalem and restore the Temple, to destroy the "wicked rule" (that is, the Roman empire), to bestow his mercy on devout proselytes and to suppress all heresy and schism. In this connection Christianity is expressly mentioned in some versions of the prayer. "May the Nazarenes perish in a moment. May they be blotted out from the book of life and not be enrolled among the just." It is significant that this clause and several like it should ever have been added without any sense that they were incongruous. Who can imagine some cry of vengeance or ill-will appended to the Lord's Prayer? There have been many vindictive sects in Christendom, but this would be quite beyond their ingenuity. To those who offered the Jewish prayer it appeared natural to throw in petitions that God, in his love for his people, should annihilate their enemies. From this alone it is evident that this prayer, in many ways so lofty, is essentially different from that of Jesus. While it seems at times to anticipate his very language it moves in quite another region of thought.

The resemblances, however, are too close to be due to mere coincidence. They no doubt arise, in some measure, from the inherent nature of prayer. There are some needs of which all men are conscious and which they cannot but speak of when they pray. It is evident, too, that the Jewish prayer was suggested by the Old Testament, and Jesus may have drawn directly from the same source. But his prayer is constructed in much the same manner as the Jewish one. The ideas follow each other in a similar order. The words employed are sometimes identically the same. It may be noted, too, that in the longer prayer, as in the *Kaddish,* the hallowing of God's name leads at once to the thought of the Kingdom, and Jesus also brings these two petitions together. What he offers is certainly no mere copy or epitome of the synagogue prayer. We feel everywhere that he is using no conventional phrases but utters thoughts and desires which have sprung out of his own heart. Short as it is, his prayer is no bare abstract of what has elsewhere been said more fully. On the contrary, it contains far more in a few simple words than all the eloquence of the Eighteen Benedictions.

It may be that Jesus was not fully conscious of his debt to the prayers of the synagogue. He had been acquainted with them all his life and their language came to him naturally when he was expressing his own thought. In our ordinary conversation we are always using phrases from the Bible or from some well-known poet, without any recollection of where we found them. They have become so much a part of our ordinary speech that we could not put certain ideas in any other way. So Jesus when he prayed may hardly have been aware that he was adopting words and phrases from the Jewish prayers. He was expressing his own thought of God and of man's relation to him, and could not but do so in the customary language of prayer. Nevertheless we have to recognise that he used that language, and may have done so purposely. He made his new prayer out of materials which had been given him.

As he fell back on the prayers of the synagogue he also availed himself of others, several of which can be identified with a fair degree of certainty. This is particularly true of the morning and evening prayers which are still included in the Jewish liturgy, and which can be traced back to the time of Jesus. There is a passage, contained in both of them, which was clearly in his mind when he made his prayer.

> Give me a portion in thy Law and lead my feet into the power of thy commandment, and lead not my feet into the power of a transgression. Bring me not into the power of a sin, nor into the power of a temptation, nor into the power of evil.

Jesus must daily have repeated these morning and evening prayers, and we cannot wonder that he echoes their words. But here again he need not have consciously borrowed. He was making a prayer which his followers were to offer every day, and could not but mention one danger from which they had daily to be guarded. He spoke of it naturally in terms which were familiar both to himself and them. The Jewish parallel, however, is here of real assistance in the understanding of the Lord's Prayer. The petition "lead us not into temptation" has always been a perplexing one, and the Jewish prayer throws a light on it. A question also has often been raised as to whether the word "evil" in the last petition should be taken abstractly or personally—"from wickedness" or "from the wicked one." The older prayer would seem to indicate a reference to evil in the general sense.

Other similarities have been discovered by diligent search into the Jewish devotional literature, but at best they are of secondary importance. Most of the passages adduced belong to periods long subsequent to the time of Jesus, and they can nearly all be explained as variants or adaptations of the more ancient prayers. If they prove anything it is that Jesus was not dependent on set models. He made use of ideas which were embedded in all Jewish religious thinking, and turned them to his own purpose. His prayer was not a patch-work of prayers which lay ready to his hand but was the spontaneous expression of what he himself felt and believed. The existing prayers served only to suggest to him how he might put his own thought into language.

This is apparent when we observe the differences between his prayer and those others to which it bears some resemblance. Later on we shall have to consider them more closely but there are some which must at once be obvious to everybody. His prayer is brief and pointed, while in the others the meaning is half lost in a mist of words. We can feel that he is really speaking to God, and knows what he desires from him. Again, the Jewish prayers never rise above the national level. The worshipper is not allowed to forget for a moment that he belongs to a chosen race, and when he addresses God as "Father" he only makes a proud assertion of the peculiar rights of his people. "Beloved of God are the Israelites," says the great Rabbi Akiba, "so that they are called the sons of God." Much is said of God's goodness and providence in those ancient prayers but it must always be remembered that they are made only on behalf of Israel as opposed to other nations. "Be merciful to thy chosen people; keep it united within itself and deliver it from its enemies." This is the real burden of those prayers which appear at first sight to anticipate that of Jesus. Again, it is taken for granted that God's demands are laid down explicitly in the Law. The aim of the prayers is to ensure that Israel as the people of God will be constant in their observance of his Law, which is their sure guide and protection. A time will come when his will is acknowledged everywhere, but this will of God is nothing else than the prescriptions set forth in the Law.

There is thus a radical difference in motive between the Lord's Prayer and the prayers of the synagogue. It is assumed in the Jewish prayers that God will bestow certain benefits on condition that his commandments are strictly obeyed. The worshipper, therefore, prays for more knowledge of the Law and for willingness to live by it; he confesses that he has sinned against it and asks to be forgiven. The idea is always that men must comply with the definite demands which God has laid on them in order to secure his benefits. In the Lord's Prayer the emphasis is all on inward harmony with God. We are to pray, not so much for the gifts of God, as for a disposition of our own which will in some manner resemble that of God. He requires of us, not that we should blindly obey him, but that we should co-operate with him, making his will our own. There is one sentence in the Lord's Prayer for which no parallel can be found in the Jewish liturgies. It is that which is conjoined with the petition "Forgive us our trespasses"; in so praying we must add "as we also forgive those who trespass against us." By this act of our own we do as God himself does, and so enable him to help us. Men have always felt that this is the real purpose of the Lord's prayer. When they repeat it they may have in mind some particular gift which they urgently require from God, but they are seeking for more than that. They wish to put themselves right with God, to see things as he sees them, to conform their own will to his will. The prayer can be offered by all men in any circumstances because the thing they ask for is to act in their own lives as God himself would do.

This is no doubt the reason why some of the main themes of the Jewish prayers are hardly touched on. Nothing is said of repentance, although we know that Jesus based his message of the Kingdom on a call to repentance. But we cannot by mere words assure God that we have truly repented. There must be a change in our condition of mind, as in that of the prodigal when he returned to his father.

In that parable, as in the prayer, the word repentance is never mentioned, but it takes the form of an act. The prayer likewise is an act, declaring, when it is sincerely prayed, that we have now a right attitude to God and a full sense of our need for him. The confession of repentance is of the very essence of the prayer. In like manner nothing is expressly said of thanksgiving. This is one of the essential elements of prayer, and its absence from this prayer, which is meant to be a pattern for all others, may indeed seem remarkable. The Psalms all turn on the theme that men must praise God for his goodness. Each petition in the great prayer of the synagogue is closed with a benediction, a thankful acknowledgment of God's past mercy. We read ever and again in the Gospels how Jesus himself gave thanks to God, and in the church that grew up after his death the very name for prayer was *"eucharistia,"* thanksgiving. Why is it that in the prayer he taught his disciples this element is wanting? It cannot be from any oversight, for in the prayers which he knew and on which he modelled his own, the central thing was the expression of thanks. Nor can it be that he purposely confined himself to petition, for the prayer begins with words of pure adoration, and this is the note throughout. There is no formal thanksgiving, for the thing itself is implicit in every word of the prayer. It gives utterance to a perfect trust in God, and in that trust we show our gratitude, not in mere words but in a mind submissive to his will. A child has confidence in his parents, and this is his way of thanking them, and they do not wish to be thanked in any other way. And what God desires of us is a gratitude which declares itself in trust. Rightly considered, this whole prayer, addressed to our Father in heaven, is one of thanksgiving.

We must allow, then, for the Old Testament and the later

Jewish influences which have gone to the making of the Lord's Prayer. There is hardly anything in it which cannot in some degree be explained by them. But its real background must be sought in Jesus' own teaching. The parallels which have been laboriously collected from alien religions and from Jewish liturgies and sayings of the Rabbis are for the most part misleading. They cause us to look at the prayer in a context which was foreign to it and so to miss its meaning. This applies even to those words and ideas which Jesus has taken directly from the Old Testament. With him they no longer signify what they did to the prophets who first used them, and the most careful study of the ancient scriptures can throw little light on what he himself said. Their meaning in his prayer cannot be understood unless we relate them to his own message.

Matthew has thus shown a true perception when he presents the prayer as an integral part of the Sermon on the Mount. It is not probable that Jesus threw it out, almost incidentally, in the course of a long address. It stands by itself, and he must have devoted much time and thought to the making of it. Yet his aim was to gather up in it the fundamental elements of all his teaching. He meant that it should be interpreted in the light of those new truths he had been impressing on his disciples. Whenever they repeated it they were to recall the many things he had taught them, by act and saying and parable. These would explain what was now compressed into a few brief sentences. Matthew has perceived this connection between the prayer and the teaching generally, and has therefore given it a place right in the middle of the Sermon on the Mount.

We do not know at what time in the ministry the prayer was given, but it cannot have been at the very outset. Jesus assumes that the disciples are now familiar with the main principles of his thought. He does not need to state anything in detail, for a single word will be enough to suggest all the ideas involved in it. The prayer at first sight may appear bare and fragmentary, and a theory has been put forward that originally it was much fuller and that only a few notes of it have been preserved. This view is certainly mistaken. While the prayer is short it has all the completeness of a work of art, and we know that one of the objects of Jesus was to illustrate his principle that prayer should be utterly simple and direct. In so far as it is only an outline this was intended by Jesus, for he wished to sum up in brief compass all that he had taught. While praying in his name, men were to remember his whole message and so fill up for themselves the outline of his prayer.

This is evident when we look at the petitions one by one. Each of them is like a condensed statement of things which have elsewhere been fully explained. It would be possible to draw up an account of all the Gospel teaching under the various heads provided by the Lord's Prayer. It centres in the petition "Thy Kingdom come," and these words, taken by themselves, have little meaning. Something like them may indeed be found frequently in Jewish prayers, but when we consider only this background, the Kingdom is nothing more than a future condition of things when the God of Israel will be acknowledged everywhere, and will reign through his chosen people. Jesus had his own conception of the Kingdom, and his teaching is mainly occupied with expounding it. He thinks of it as the coming time when men's standards will all be changed, when all will know God as their Father and will make it their one endeavour to do his will. So when Jesus bade us pray for the Kingdom he wished us to conceive of it as he himself did. We are to remember the blessings he pronounced on the meek, and the merciful and the pure in heart; the parables in which he taught that only through love and humility and self-sacrifice can we enter the Kingdom. Nothing of this is expressly said in the prayer, but all would be clear to those who had listened to him and had seen him in action. They would know what he meant by the Kingdom and how he required them to live and work for it. This is still necessary if the prayer is to be rightly offered. It carries with it not only what it directly says but all that it suggests to us from our whole knowledge of the teaching.

What is true of the petition for the Kingdom is equally true of all the others. They have to be interpreted from what we know of the mind of Jesus as it was revealed in everything that he said and did. Nothing can be more fatal than to leave Jesus himself out of his prayer and to lay all the stress on what he apparently borrowed from prayers already existing. This has sometimes been done, with the result that there seems to be nothing new in the prayer and nothing that is not vague and general. It is largely for this reason that the saying of it is so often little more than a pious gesture. If the words convey any meaning to those who so utter them it is only that our lives depend on God and that we ought to honour him. There is a value certainly even in this, but we miss the true import of the prayer unless we think of it as speaking the mind of Jesus. By means of it he expressed his own faith in God, his own conception of what God requires from men. It cannot be separated from his message as a whole.

So it is by the teaching that we must understand the prayer, and it is also the prayer that illuminates the teaching. This was no doubt part of Jesus' intention when he made it. Paul speaks of "the simplicity of Christ," and when we compare the Gospels with the writings of any religious or philosophical thinker, or with the Epistles of Paul himself, we are struck most of all with the limpid clearness of everything that Jesus said. The common people heard him gladly, for he made his meaning plain even to the most ignorant. He spoke nothing without a parable, illustrating his thought from facts and experiences which were known to all. Nothing could be more perfectly simple than the teaching of Jesus, and yet it is difficult, more difficult than any other. It has been expounded by countless theologians, who have often been accused of needlessly complicating what he had expressed so clearly, but their aim has been to simplify. For when men began to reflect on the thought of Jesus they found that it reached down to depths which they could not fathom, and they have sought, with all the resources of human intellect, to make out at least some little part of what was involved in those sayings which seem to be so transparent. There is no prospect that this effort to explore the thought of Jesus will ever end.

He was himself conscious that his teaching was difficult. It was only too evident to him that even his disciples were making little of what he said, while to the world at large his message was unintelligible. But he meant his prayer to supply a key to it. For one thing it fixed the mind on a few plain truths which would serve as land-marks to those who might feel bewildered. In the course of his teaching he had occasion to deal with a great variety of subjects. There is hardly any human interest on which he does not touch in one or another of his sayings, and the attempt has often been made to collect and tabulate them and so construct a sort of guide-book for Christian conduct in all the perplexing duties of life. This always results in confusion. We can all think of men who have tried to act literally on every precept of Jesus, only to bring misery on themselves and others. He saw that this might happen, and left us his prayer to keep us in the right road. Much of his teaching might be difficult, but here were the primary truths on which all the rest depended. God is over the world and is working towards the fulfilment of his eternal purpose. We must have a living trust in God, and bring our lives into harmony with his will. We must be merciful as God is, and resist every form of evil. So in his prayer Jesus set forth the guiding principles of his religion. We are to keep them in our memory and hold fast to them, and if we do so we cannot go far wrong. All that might perplex us in his teaching will gradually explain itself.

He thus gave his prayer to his community as the standing test of those who had a right to belong to it. What is it that makes a Christian? This is a question which has troubled the church from the very beginning, and it has commonly been answered by drawing up a creed or confession to which all would-be members had to assent. Jesus did not do this. He only made a prayer which his followers had to repeat together. Those who could sincerely join in it declared themselves thereby to be of his company. Whatever might be their differences of opinion they were at one with him in essential things. Repeating his prayer they accepted his teaching and expressed their desire to live by it. This was Jesus' own test of discipleship and it is still valid. We cannot deny the name of Christian to any one who can join, with his whole heart, in the Lord's Prayer.

It was the custom in old churches to have the Ten Commandments and the Lord's Prayer hung up on the wall side by side in front of the worshippers, and they are indeed the counterparts of each other. The Law was made up of hundreds of separate rules, but the substance of them was all contained in those Commandments, given to Moses on the

Mount. The Christian teaching is manifold, but its requirements all branch out from the Lord's Prayer. It may be said, too, that the prayer and the Commandments have the same general import. They both seek to impress on us that we belong to God and must obey his will, which is one of righteousness. But there is one vital difference between them, and it is marked out by the fact that one is a series of commandments and the other is a prayer. On the one hand the will of God is imposed on us from without; on the other we desire ourselves to know it and make it our own. The aim of Jesus was to change the hearts of men, so that trusting God they should serve him willingly, and work along with him for the fulfilment of his purpose. This was the motive of all the teaching of Jesus, and he makes it clear to us in his prayer.

CHAPTER IV

THE ORIGINALITY OF THE PRAYER

THERE is hardly anything in the Lord's Prayer for which some parallel cannot be found in earlier religion. Some of the petitions are repeated almost literally from prayers which were already in constant use. The question arises, therefore, whether there is anything original in this prayer of Jesus. He gave it to his disciples as the very symbol of their new beliefs, and yet, when we examine it closely, there seems to be little in it that men had not been saying thousands of times before.

We need to consider, however, what we mean when we call anything original. On this point there is much confusion of thought, which is working incalculable harm in our time. We claim to be living in a new age, and have grown impatient of anything that is not new. Statesmen, writers, artists, thinkers are all striving to be original and imagine that they attain this end when they are merely eccentric and absurd. The truth is that there can be nothing that is strictly original. Men have been living on this earth for ages, and at one time or another have tried everything, and have learned by hard experience what they ought to do. They have found that some principles are inherent in the nature of things, and that all goes wrong when these are put aside. Originality consists, not in breaking away from these principles but in a deeper understanding of them. In themselves they are as old as time, but since they survive all changes there must be something in them deeper than we yet know. It is the very mark of an original man that what he does appears to be perfectly natural. His poem goes to your heart because it touches an emotion you have felt yourself. His theory impresses you as the right one because it is borne out by everyday facts. Plato maintained that knowledge, in the last resort, is a process of recollection. Truth which we have learned in some previous state of being is slumbering in our minds, and our thought and experience serve only to awaken it. The idea may be fantastic but this at least is certain, that all advance in knowledge involves a going back, from things on the surface to things further down, from passing experiences to abiding principles. The original mind is that which can discover the old beneath the new.

Most of all in religion this is the only true meaning of originality. The whole object of religion is to lay hold of that which is everlasting. This does not mean that modes of worship and belief must never vary. If religion is to keep alive it must ever be changing, as all living things must do. But through the changes it must be striving to free itself from that which is only temporary and accidental and so reach back to that which does not change. The men whom we associate with the great advances in religious history have never been innovators. On the contrary they have protested, and rightly so, that they were only going back to the past. They have taken their stand on some ancient truth which has been forgotten or obscured. They have turned away from later novelties to the word of scripture, to the example of the primitive church, to the teaching of Jesus himself. Their aim has been to recover a truth which has always been present beneath the errors which have crept in from time to time. This has been their originality. They gave something new because they had deeper insight into that which was old.

It is in this light that we must understand the newness of the Lord's Prayer. If it had contained nothing that had been said before it would not have been a prayer, for in prayer we seek to remind ourselves of things which are always the same. There is nothing in this world that endures, so we look beyond it to the eternal God. Our minds keep shifting to new projects, but we try to fix them on the abiding purposes of life. Prayer by its nature is concerned with the permanent things, and men have always been aware of them, and have spoken of them in much the same way. Jesus could not have devised an entirely new prayer, and had no desire to do so. He sought rather to make it plain that what he now said was only the substance of what men had always been praying. He took up the very language in which his disciples had been accustomed to pray and thus reminded them that the fundamental needs of man's nature are always the same.

The prayer thus illustrates his own profound saying, "Think not that I have come to destroy the law and the prophets; I am not come to destroy but to fulfil." He had brought a new revelation but it only disclosed what had been implicit in the old one. When we follow out this idea we can see in it the inner principle which governs the whole course of nature and of human history. There is never any destruction but only an unfolding. The old gives place to something which appears to be new but is only the fuller growth of what was there already, the flower which was hidden in the seed. Nothing ever perishes but only passes into fulfilment. In his prayer Jesus gives concrete expression to this principle of which he was aware. He had to make a new prayer for his community but took care that it should not be altogether a different one. He had not come to destroy the Law and the prophets, and if much of his prayer appears to be borrowed from them this was his intention. He sought as far as possible to preserve the existing prayers, to draw out of them what was of lasting value and so to fulfil them.

In what sense, then, was the prayer original? When it is put side by side with the Jewish prayers we are indeed struck with the resemblance but still more with the difference. It says perfectly what the others are trying to say. It brings us, as they fail to do, into an immediate relation to God. It says less and yet infinitely more. If there has ever been an original utterance it is this prayer of Jesus, which has transformed the whole meaning of prayer, and given us a new conception of God and his purposes with man. Why does it bear this stamp of originality although so much of it is old?

For one thing, Jesus does not merely repeat the older prayers but makes his own selection from them. They had contained much that was true and precious but this was mingled, almost hopelessly, with baser metal. In offering them men had been divided in their minds. They had asked God for his heavenly gifts while all the time they were bound to this world, and were seeking their own advantage or that of their particular tribe or nation. They confounded the purpose of God with some party enterprise, often of a very doubtful character. Even in the loftiest of the Psalms there is almost always some jarring note of this kind, and the same is true of the later prayers. The higher and the lower interests are tangled together in such a way that sometimes they can hardly be distinguished. This is commonly forgotten when parallels are sought to the prayer of Jesus. It is easy to point to some things he has preserved but we have also to consider what he has discarded. A sculptor finds his statue in the block of marble, but only by chipping away all parts of it that are useless to his design. His art consists in shaping the rough material to the idea which is in his own mind. Much the same may be said of Jesus' prayer as compared with the prayers before him. He selects from them in such a manner as to make something altogether new.

But the prayer is much more than a selection, however skilfully made. The borrowed petitions are not merely strung together, each one standing by itself, as in an anthology of poems or proverbs. They are all so remodelled as to bring out their essential meaning, and are placed in organic relation to one another. In the older prayers there is little or no coherence. The Eighteen Benedictions grew up, as we have seen, over a long period, and a new sentence was tacked on to the others from time to time, as occasion required. If the worshipper was not at leisure he might pick out a clause or two at random, and could feel that they were sufficient by themselves. No one could deal in this way with the Lord's Prayer. The more closely we examine it the more we find that it all of a piece, each sentence depending on the one before and the one after. It is not a series of petitions but a single prayer, all springing naturally out of the same root. Men had always been conscious of many needs, widely different from each other, and had been content to name them separately as they waited on God. Jesus perceived that while the needs were different they all hung together. In the last resort we have only one great need, and the Lord's Prayer loses its meaning unless it is taken as a whole.

It is thus assumed in the prayer that while man's life has many aspects it is all a unity, and Jesus was the first who had this conception of it. All previous thought had taken for granted that two different beings were strangely compounded in man. He was a creature of this earth, similar to the beasts that perish, and was yet in some manner allied to God. According to many ancient teachers the divine element had strayed into him by some accident or mistake, and his task was to liberate it by mortifying the flesh and holding aloof from all earthly interests. According to others the two sides of our nature were to be kept separate but so controlled as to work together harmoniously. Plato in a famous passage compares man to a charioteer driving two horses, each of them struggling to pull away from the other. This idea of the duality of man's being has never lost its hold. We feel that whether we will or not we must serve two masters. We sharply divide the sacred from the secular, and it makes us uneasy when the one intrudes on the other. Jesus broke down this distinction. He indeed thought of this world as subject to Satan, but never doubted that this was a usurpation which must come to an end. The world belongs wholly to God, and although its interests are only for a time they are ordained by him to serve his higher purpose. In all that they do men are occupied with sacred things which they must so use as to offer a continual service to God.

This idea of the wholeness of man's being is reflected in the Lord's Prayer. Jesus regards our life, not as consisting of two parts, but as turning on two poles. It aspires to that which is eternal but is directly concerned with that which is earthly, and these two aspects of it must not be kept apart. The prayer, it may be said, is pivoted on the two petitions: "Thy Kingdom come," and "Give us to-day our daily bread." You are to look to the future Kingdom, in which the things of time will all be forgotten, and yet ask God to sustain you through the passing day. There have been religions, like those of India, which have taught that nothing matters but the eternal realities. There have been others, as in Greece and China, which have laid all stress on present action. To-day is ours and we can throw ourselves wholly into its duties, as if our life were wholly compressed into these few hours. There is profound truth in both of these conceptions, but each of them is false without the other. The man who lives only for the eternal loses the brief time which is his sure possession; he does not really live at all. The man who lives only for the day is likewise wasting himself. His strenuous action goes for nothing, since it is not directed to any purpose. It is done for the moment and will die with it. The true life is that which is mindful of God and his Kingdom, and yet makes the most of every day that comes and goes. The two conceptions do not exclude each other, for neither of them has value unless they go hand in hand. For Jesus, therefore, each day is like a step forward on a journey. It seems in itself to be only an idle motion, but it is making towards the goal, and the thought of this must be present in your mind as you take it. The earthly life is the road to the eternal. By impressing this truth on men Jesus gave a new character to religion, and it dominates the Lord's Prayer. Almost in one breath we are to pray for the Kingdom of God and for his help in living this single day.

The prayer is original not only when viewed as a whole but in all its several parts. It seems to be made up of borrowed words and phrases but this appearance of it is deceptive, and by interpreting it at any point by the Jewish parallels we miss its meaning altogether. Jesus employed old language to convey his new ideas, as every discoverer is compelled to do. The astronomer calls the stars by the names given them long ago, when nothing was known of their nature and motions. The reformer speaks of liberty and civil rights, but understands them in a sense which was never contemplated in Magna Charta. The poet employs common words but puts something into them which no one imagined before him. So Jesus availed himself of the ordinary language of prayer, but we have always to enquire what it meant to himself. This we must do in the light of his whole teaching, and not only of his teaching but of his life and death. By our knowledge of his own mind and not of any ancient parallels we must understand his prayer.

When we so examine it we can see that in language which he has borrowed he is saying things which were entirely new. Almost every word implies a thought or an attitude of mind which had not been possible to any one before him. Take the words "Our Father," familiar to every worshipper in the synagogue. When Jesus uttered them he was not thinking of a chosen race which claimed to stand in a special relation to God. He spoke for all humanity, and in the name "Father" he gathered up everything he had taught of God's love and compassion, and of his care for each one of his children. The prayer goes on to tell of the holiness of God, and Jesus conceived of it in a quite different way from those who honoured it by ritual and sacrifice. He prayed "Thy Kingdom come," and here, too, we must remember what he had himself said about the Kingdom—why we should desire it, and how it would come, and who would enter into it. So in the petitions for forgiveness and deliverance from temptation and evil we need to put ourselves into the mind of Jesus. How did he think of forgiveness?

What were the temptations against which he sought to warn us? At every point in the prayer we cannot but feel that old words have acquired a new meaning. We look out, as it were, in the morning on a scene we have passed through in the dark. Everything is the same but a veil has been lifted, and each object is now distinct, and there is order and beauty where all was in confusion. The originality of Jesus has often been called in question. All ancient literatures have been ransacked to discover analogies to his sayings, and it cannot be denied that here and there he had been anticipated. This was inevitable, for great moral and religious truths have always been manifest and he could not but repeat what wise men had said already. He took words which had hitherto conveyed little meaning and made them expressive of the very greatest things.

When we compare his prayer with the earlier ones we are struck most of all with its universality. The Jewish prayers, beautiful as they often are, do not reach beyond the nation. God is the Father of Israel; the blessings sought from him are for those whom he has specially chosen. In the prayers of all the old religions we are conscious of the same narrowness of outlook. It is assumed as self-evident that God cares only for those who have a definite claim upon him and worship him in one particular way. In the Lord's Prayer there is nothing exclusive. It rests on the conviction that God is the Father of all men and that they must wait on him with those great human needs which are common to all. It has been argued, largely on the ground of this prayer, that there was nothing remarkable in the work of Jesus. A lofty ethical religion had grown up in Israel but had so far been restricted to the one people. All that Jesus did was to break down the barriers, so that the world at large might share in what had been held as a monopoly. Sooner or later, we are told, the extension was bound to come, much as the art of printing or the parliamentary system which began in one country was gradually adopted by the others. Jesus merely hastened an inevitable process. But the natural process was just the opposite one. Judaism indeed developed in line with its inherent character, and instead of widening became ever narrower. The national idea was of its very essence, and it was not Jesus but the Pharisees who stood for its true destiny. His work did not consist in enlarging and improving the old religion but in changing it at its very centre. He made men think quite differently about God, and man's relation to him, and the whole purpose of human life.

So the prayer is universal because it takes account of men simply as men. Not only so, but it goes down to what is deepest in man's nature and makes him man. It was thus in the very fullest sense original. It cast aside the conceptions which were fundamental to all prayers before it and replaced them with others which were entirely new. Paul was well acquainted with those Jewish prayers from which Jesus is supposed to have borrowed, but when he tries to fix on the essential difference between the old religion and the new he contrasts the two modes of prayer. "Ye have not received the spirit of bondage again to fear, but ye have received the Spirit of adoption whereby we cry Abba, Father." Here, as we have seen, he quotes the opening invocation of the Lord's Prayer, on which all Christian prayer was modelled. He finds in this prayer the surest evidence that Christianity was a new religion, distinct from all others. The essential act in religion is prayer, and the people of Christ, praying as he had taught them, can do so in a new state of mind, under a different impulse.

In two respects Paul draws a contrast between the Christian prayer and those which had been offered hitherto. On the one hand the older prayers had arisen from "a spirit of bondage." Men had approached God as underlings, afraid of how he might receive them. They had favours to ask of him, and perhaps he might be well disposed and throw them some little gift out of his bounty. Perhaps he might be angry at their presumption and drive them from his presence. A feeling of this kind is always discernible behind the ancient prayers. They may be earnest and moving but the worshipper thinks of God as an arbitrary master, of whose good will he never can be certain, and who will give grudgingly if he gives at all. In Christian prayer there is none of this sense of bondage. You indeed acknowledge that God is far above you but you call him Father. He has adopted you into his own family. You can tell him freely of all your wants, and if he does not grant them you can still trust in his goodness. He is wiser than you are and knows what you require. This is the attitude of mind which finds expression in the Lord's Prayer and which makes it different in its very substance from all prayers which had been offered before.

On the other hand Paul speaks of a power which prays along with you. The Spirit teaches you what you should pray for and supports you in your petition. Paul here describes, in theological language, a fact of common experience. Genuine Christian prayer is always accompanied with an inward glow. The person who utters it is lifted out of himself. He feels that there is an impelling force behind him which gives weight and significance to what he says. Not only so, but he prays with a sense of certainty. What he desires may seem impossible but there is something within him which tells him that it will be granted. Jesus also declares that in true prayer all doubts are swept away. You have such confidence in God that you believe that what you ask for, however bold may be your petition, you will receive.

This confidence is the prevailing note of the Lord's Prayer. There is nothing in it that suggests a mood of ecstasy. It consists of a few brief sentences, with a pause after each of them to allow time for reflection. No one can imagine the Lord's Prayer repeated to the accompaniment of wild cries and exciting music. It draws you back into yourself and you say it quietly to the Father who sees in secret. But the Spirit manifests itself, as Paul was ever reminding his concerts, not only in miracles and speaking with tongues, but in faith and love and the inward assurance of God. Behind the Lord's Prayer there is the certainty that God is real, that he knows and cares for us, that he requires us to do his will. The tranquillity of the prayer is due to nothing else than a perfect reliance on God, and we have this confidence through a power which is not our own. "Because ye are sons God hath sent forth the Spirit of his Son into your hearts, crying Abba, Father."

Paul thus points us to the ultimate reason why the prayer is original. It is modelled on prayers which were already familiar to everybody, but Jesus added something which was entirely his own. He made ancient words express his new conception of the nature of God. He made them the vehicle also of his own unquestioning faith. As we repeat the prayer we no longer think of God as remote and inaccessible. We know as Christians that while he is invisible he is yet near, and is guiding and sustaining us in our daily lives. This is what we value in the prayer. Men have always been conscious of the needs expressed in it, and in earlier prayers they had called on God to help them. Jesus took up the old petitions, for he could not do otherwise if he was to speak for suffering men. But he brought the assurance that God would indeed pity and help. In praying to him we are not merely throwing words into the air, hoping wistfully that there is someone who will hear. We believe that when we speak to God he will answer us. Jesus taught us to pray with his own certainty of the presence and the goodness of God. Whatever he may have borrowed he gave this out of himself, and it is the new and vital element in his prayer.

It is thus profoundly original, and we have here the surest token of its authenticity. Some modern scholars have argued that it was only an early Christian prayer which came to be attributed to Jesus himself. This view is bound up with the general theory that little was remembered of Jesus after his death, and that the church employed his name to give sanction to its own practices and beliefs. Among other things there was a prayer which had somehow sprung up in the Christian meetings, and the idea gained ground that Jesus himself had given it. A great deal is made of the fact that it has come down to us in two versions which at some points differ from each other. Does this not indicate that it was of doubtful origin, and had no place in the earliest tradition? But the inference that must be drawn is just the contrary. It is now an accepted principle in all enquiry that when two things are alike and yet different they must have had a common root. Diverging species of plant or animal point back to one, now perhaps extinct, from which they have all sprung. Languages which vary widely and are yet similar bear witness to one language behind them all. Records which contradict each other but are broadly in agreement are evidence of something that really happened. Modern science is all built on this principle that when there is likeness under variation you can reach back to a common origin. We have two accounts of the Lord's Prayer, but the very fact that they differ makes their agreement the more significant. They must be records of the same prayer, and if they vary this only proves that it must have been so long in existence that differences had crept in. When we remember that Matthew and Luke wrote their Gospels only fifty or sixty years after Jesus' death and make use of records which had arisen much earlier, we are taken back almost to the beginning of the church. From the outset it had offered a prayer which it believed to be the work of Jesus, and which never ceased to be essentially the same.

But the authenticity of the prayer does not rest on mere critical evidences. In its very substance it bears the signature of Jesus and can be attributed to no one else. For one thing it must have originated in Palestine, and in the time when Jesus lived. Its language is that of the synagogue of his day. Its ideas are in keeping with those which were in the air around him. The theory that it grew up in the later church is quite inconceivable. We know the character of the early Christian prayers, many of which are preserved in the New Testament. They all centre on beliefs which were held by Jesus' followers only after he had departed; that he was the promised Messiah, that he was presently to come again, that those who confessed him would share in his Resurrection, that he was now acting through his church and the Spirit which he had sent. Almost from the hour that he left them these beliefs possessed the minds of his disciples, and out of them the church arose. It would not have been possible for any Christian in that after time to frame a prayer which did not in some manner turn on them. Yet in the Lord's Prayer, composed, it is argued, by the early church, as its confession of faith, they are never even suggested. We have seen that in Luke's version the petition "Thy Kingdom come" was sometimes changed into "May thy Spirit come upon us and cleanse us." Here we can indeed see the hand of the church, and the whole prayer would have been of

similar character if it had been made in that later age. But
it remained as it was, for no other possible reason than that
Jesus himself had so taught it.

Again, it answers, in every detail, to Jesus' own conception of prayer. He spoke on this theme in many different
connections and described in the fullest terms what a true
prayer ought to be. It should be brief and simple and direct.
In offering it we must rid ourselves of all pretence and remember that God sees into our hearts. Before venturing to
pray to God we must be reconciled to our fellow-men. By
these instructions Jesus put the whole method of prayer on
a new footing. Not only among the Jews but in all religions
of that age it was assumed that men would be heard for
their much speaking. Prayers were vague and conventional;
they were supposed to have value for their own sake, quite
apart from the spirit in which they were offered; they were
directed as much to the onlookers as to God. Jesus conceived
of prayer in a manner which was all his own, and the prayer
which has come down to us under his name is in perfect
harmony with his instructions. No one else in his time would
ever have thought of praying in just that way, and we cannot doubt that the voice we hear was his.

The prayer conforms also to his teaching generally. Matthew places it right in the middle of the Sermon on the
Mount because he saw in it the sum of all the sayings, expressed in the form of a prayer. For the same reason the
church in every age has made it a necessary part of all acts
of worship. It stands for the whole message of Jesus. It
reminds us of all that he taught us about God and our relation to him and the aims he has set before us and our obliga-
tions as Christian men. All this is condensed into the prayer.
It is not as if some one had carefully studied the Gospels and
drawn up a brief summary of their teaching. This has often

been attempted with the result that nothing is given us but a few dry bones. The prayer throbs with life. It presents his thought from the inside, just as he himself might have done. Who was it that could have entered so completely into his mind? In the early church there were indeed devoted Christian men, but there was no one who could have spoken in the very voice of Jesus. The prayer is so absolutely true to all his thinking and is so fresh and spontaneous that no one could have uttered it but Jesus himself.

It is this individual note in the prayer that testifies to its authenticity. Its language may be partly borrowed, but it is original in the only sense in which this term may be rightly applied to anything. The only new thing that ever enters into this world is a human personality, and an original work is one which breathes the very self of him who made it. As we repeat the Lord's Prayer we feel ourselves in contact with a personality, which is unmistakably that of Jesus. The words may be ancient but he has put into them the faith and the insight and the sympathy and the compelling power which were altogether his own. No words ever spoken have taken such a hold on men as those of the Lord's Prayer, and the ultimate reason must be sought, not so much in the words themselves as in something inexplicable which pulses in them. They convey to us the mind of Jesus and no other. He is himself present in his prayer.

Not only does it bear the intrinsic mark of authenticity, but it may fairly be regarded as the best attested of all the utterances of Jesus. His other sayings are preserved to us only by happy accident. He taught informally, and among those who listened to him there were sometimes one or two who were impressed by words he said and kept them in their memory. Once he compared himself to a sower who flung his seed broadcast, knowing that most of it would come to nothing and that only here and there it would fall on good ground. But this prayer was on a different footing from the rest of his teaching. He took care to imprint it on the minds of his disciples. He meant it to be the standard prayer which they would constantly be offering. This they have kept doing from the hour when he first spoke it to the present day. The piety of the Middle Ages was eager above all things to find some tangible relic of Jesus—a fragment of his robe, a cup he had drunk from, a splinter of the holy Cross. In the Lord's Prayer we actually possess such a relic, and by means of it we touch what was inmost in the Person of Jesus. We can feel as we repeat it that our ears have heard and our hands have handled his word of life.

CHAPTER V

THE SEVEN PETITIONS

THE Lord's Prayer is made up of a few short sentences, all of them concerned with the primary needs of life. It was clearly the intention of Jesus to reduce prayer to its simplest elements. In the religion of his time it had become wordy and complicated. It ran off into so many side-issues that men lost sight of the essential things which they required from God. Jesus taught a prayer in which there was nothing unnecessary. He wished men to fix their minds on their fundamental needs, and to tell them in the plainest words.

But while the prayer is simple it is deep and comprehensive, and this also was intended by Jesus. He made every sentence stand out boldly by itself, so that we might try to realise how much was involved in it. It is always the simple things which prove in the end to be unfathomable. Any clever man, with a little patience and ingenuity, can solve a puzzle; but who will ever explain life or love or duty or faith in God? These are the elementary facts of our being, but they are also its ultimate mysteries. Jesus sought to impress on us this significance of things we take for granted.

74

His prayer, which on the face of it is so simple, is perhaps the most baffling of all known utterances. It is difficult because it is so simple, taking us back to the great realities on which everything is based.

But the prayer has difficulties of another kind which were not intended by Jesus. For one thing, the extreme condensation of his thought has made it at some points obscure. His aim was to express great truths with the utmost brevity, but language was not equal to the strain he put on it, and we are left wondering sometimes what was in his mind. Again, we know his words only in a translation. There are phrases in the prayer which would be perfectly clear in the Aramaic which he spoke but had no proper equivalents in Greek, and we can only guess at their precise meaning. Again, the prayer is affected in some degree by ancient modes of thinking which have grown strange to us. Jesus availed himself, as we have seen, of existing Jewish prayers. He indeed put a new significance into the terms he borrowed, and it is this which has always to be considered. Nevertheless it is wrapt up in the old forms of thought, and we have to penetrate to the substance through these forms. There is hardly a sentence in which we are not faced by this difficulty.

It is necessary, therefore, to examine the prayer closely, sentence by sentence, but we must first remind ourselves again that it is an organic unity, in which every several part is related to the others. Jesus was not merely stringing together a number of man's chief requirements but was trying to make us feel that they are all connected, and that none of them can be taken all by itself. The danger of religion has always been to become one-sided. A man seeks to be morally blameless while his spiritual life is empty. He takes his stand on doctrine or pious observances and neglects his practical duties. He works for the good of others and is careless about his own soul. Most of our religion is of this partial kind, and it fails even in its limited purpose because the other things are left out of sight. Jesus has given us a prayer in which everything is included and in which all the elements are blended together. It has often been assumed that the prayer consists of two distinct parts, one of them dealing with man's relation to God and the other with his earthly struggle. But the very aim of Jesus was to wipe out this distinction. He brings all our religion into a single prayer which has to be offered as a whole. The petition for God's Kingdom is followed immediately by that for our daily bread, and this might appear to be a sudden drop from the higher plane to the lower. But in the thought of Jesus the one petition leads naturally to the other. We pray for the Kingdom which is far distant, and in the hope for it we ask God to sustain us from day to day.

The prayer, then, must be offered as a single whole, and in one sense it is not strictly a prayer. It is rather the expression of absolute trust in God, who reigns in heaven and is yet our Father, who is ever mindful of us and whose will we are meant to live by. For this reason it can be said in any circumstances. It might seem to have no bearing on the special difficulty which confronts you, but by means of it you throw yourself on God, with the certainty that he knows your need and will support and guide you. In battle and shipwreck, in sickness and bereavement, in every kind of perplexity men have repeated the Lord's Prayer, and have felt that it says everything for them. For behind the definite petitions there is the assurance of God's presence with those who trust him. Whatever may be our need we can place ourselves in his hands.

This wider reference of the prayer is apparent even in its

language. It alternates between petition and confident belief, or expresses them both together. "Give us our bread,"
"Forgive us," "Deliver us"; here we ask something of God.
But we are also to pray "Let thy name be hallowed," "Let
thy Kingdom come." "Let thy will be done." Here we do not
ask, but only state a sure conviction. God is the holy one: He
is working to bring in his Kingdom; he will establish his will
on earth. We know that our prayer will not affect God's purpose, but we look forward to its fulfilment and the thought
of it uplifts us. So throughout the prayer these two intentions merge in one another. We tell our desires to God and
we try also to understand what he desires, so that we may
conform our wills to his. This, for Jesus, is the real object of
prayer. It is not a method of obtaining from God certain
benefits which he is withholding. It is an effort, rather, to
learn what he wishes to give, so that we may accept it willingly.

We thus come to a question which has been much de-
bated. How many petitions are offered in the Lord's Prayer?
The answer depends on what we mean by a petition. If we
understand the word in a strict sense the opening sentences
may be taken as only preliminary. Before making the prayer
you put yourself into the right mood of reverence by thinking of God's majesty and his eternal purpose. Then come
the definite petitions, which are only four—for bread, forgiveness, power to resist temptation, deliverance from evil.
The number would rise to six if "Thy Kingdom come" and
"Thy will be done" are reckoned as petitions, but it is possible that these two should be taken together, the second
merely defining the first. "Bring in thy Kingdom, the new
order in which everything will be subject to thy will." This
is how the prayer is understood in Luke's version, and "Thy
will be done" is left out. In like manner the final petition

"Deliver us from evil" is omitted, since it appears to be merely a duplicate of the one before it, "Lead us not into temptation." It is not surprising, therefore, that there is much diversity of opinion as to the number of the petitions. Reasons may be given for making it three, four, five, six or seven.

We may be certain, however, that there is nothing redundant in the prayer. The express aim of Jesus was to avoid all "vain repetitions" and to ensure that when you pray to God you should put a meaning into every word you utter. He would never have loaded his prayer with anything that could be left out. We shall see when we examine them more closely that the two clauses which Luke omits are no mere variations of what had been said already. Moreover, the whole attempt to limit the number of petitions is based on a misunderstanding. It assumes that the prayer falls into two parts and that the first consists wholly of words of adoration, which must be distinguished from actual prayer. But in the mind of Jesus there was no such distinction. Prayer, as he conceived it, is the act of communion with God. The object of it is not so much to obtain gifts at his hand as to learn his will and bring our own into harmony with it. The whole prayer, therefore, is made up of petitions, and the most important of them are those which stand at the beginning. We there pray for a true knowledge of God and of his purpose, for without this we cannot rightly pray for anything. There are thus seven petitions in the prayer. It has been held that Jesus adopted this as the sacred number, but his mind did not move in any mechanical way. Least of all when he was teaching men to pray with utter sincerity would he frame his prayer on an artificial plan. His one aim was to choose out the essential human needs, and he fixed on these seven.

The opening invocation is not to be reckoned among the petitions, but they all spring out of it, like branches from the stem. In all centuries the prayer has been known as the "*Pater noster*," the "Our Father," and when Paul says that Christians pray "Abba, Father," he may already have this title in his mind. The prayer was called from its opening words, not only because they were the first, but because they were felt to be the most significant. They tell us how we must think of God, and the petitions which follow all proceed, in a logical order, from this knowledge of who he is. We pray first that while we call him our Father we may yet reverence him as high above this world. Then we assure ourselves that in his government of the world he has a great purpose which he will at last fulfil, and which he is fulfilling even now. Then we think of our own lives as ordered by God. He sustains us from day to day. We offend against him but trust that he will forgive us, guard us henceforth from temptation, and deliver us from every kind of evil. Thus the petitions spring almost of their own accord, each one from the one before it and all of them from the confidence that the eternal God is our Father and that our earthly life is mysteriously bound up with him.

It must never be forgotten that the prayer is at once communal and individual. Jesus meant it to be repeated in unison by his followers, who were thus to signify that they were brethren, all dedicated to his new way of life. According to Luke they had themselves asked for such a prayer, reminding him that John the Baptist had made a special prayer for his disciples. No record of John's prayer has survived, but Luke was evidently acquainted with it, and saw in it some resemblance to the prayer of Jesus. No doubt it touched on the outstanding themes of John's teaching—his proclamation that the Kingdom of God was at hand, his call to repentance, his demand for practical and not merely formal religion. At some points it would coincide with the prayer of Jesus, but with this difference, that John was the leader of a sect while the interests of Jesus were universal. The community he had in mind was one which looked to what was ultimate and abiding in man's relation to God. As yet it was only a tiny brotherhood but potentially it embraced all mankind.

He thought, therefore, of a company of people, united in their aims and sympathies, who were to repeat this prayer together. It speaks in the plural of our Father, our daily bread, our trespasses. It consists of brief, pointed sentences which every one could easily learn by heart. It lends itself by its half-rhythmical language to being chanted by a number of voices. But while it is the prayer of a community it is individual in its whole spirit and purpose. Each person who utters it is compelled to think of his own aspirations, his own troubles and shortcomings and needs. This was certainly the intention of Jesus. When he bade us say "as we forgive those who have trespassed against us" he did not call on a church or a nation to exercise some vague corporate forgiveness. He required you and me to examine our own feelings and actions and so ask ourselves whether we have the right to be forgiven. In all the petitions it is the individual who prays. He approaches God, not in virtue of his membership in some favoured community, but because he is conscious of his own needs and knows God as his Father who will satisfy them.

The prayer is individual for the very reason that it is communal. It is concerned with those things which are essential in every man's life, and which you do not fully realise until you make yourself one with other men. While you stand apart you do not know your true self. You are wrapt up in private interests which have nothing to do with the great issues of life. In fellowship with other souls you see your own as in a mirror; you become aware of what is deepest and most real in your human nature. Many hard things have been said of the hypocrisy of public worship. A man joins himself for an hour with a devout company and expresses the loftiest hopes and convictions; but you see him next day at his ordinary business and discover what he really is. But may it not be rather the other way? Worshipping along with others he reveals his inner self, if only for that brief interval. He finds something in his being which he has never himself suspected and which is yet the essential man. The prayer of Jesus is communal because it touches what is deepest in the hearts of all men, and is therefore most personal to each one of them.

Again, while he thought of prayer as individual, spoken in secret to the Father who sees in secret, Jesus never meant it to be merely selfish. This has always been the chief danger of prayer. In dire emergencies we pray to God, conscious only of our own pressing need. It cannot well be otherwise, for prayer would lose all its value if it were not the utterance of what you most require of God in your actual life. But since this is its nature it easily becomes a form of egoism. Perhaps most prayers have no other object than to magnify the importance of ourselves and our private concerns. It has often been remarked that famous saints who devoted their whole lives to prayer have become morbidly absorbed in themselves. Their one interest was in the welfare of their own souls, and they almost forgot that God had any one else to care for. Jesus so framed his prayer that in repeating it we should remember others who are likewise God's children. Not only when we join in communal worship but in our own most intimate devotion we are to feel that we belong to a great company and must speak of "us" and "our." If we suffer we must bear in mind the sufferings of others, and the thought of them will help us in our own. If we seek a benefit from God it must be one which we are willing, in some way, to share with our fellow-men. This feeling of sympathy with those around us, even when we pray for ourselves, was for Jesus one of the primary conditions of true prayer.

From the prayer as a whole we now turn to the seven petitions of which it is composed. They need to be considered separately, but always with the consciousness that each one must be understood in the light of all the others. It is possible to make the petitions one by one and yet leave the prayer unsaid, for it consists ultimately of that knowledge of God which Jesus himself possessed and which he sought to impart to us. This is the element which gives meaning to the prayer. Taken by themselves the petitions may seem to be much the same as those which were made in the synagogue, and which were almost as old in substance as the human race. Jesus put a significance into them which is not apparent unless all of them are taken together.

The prayer begins, then, with the invocation "Our Father who art in heaven." According to the version in Luke Jesus only used the single word "Father," and it has been held that the more formal opening in Matthew was an expansion, for liturgical purposes, of the original word. It is pointed out that when Jesus himself prayed he addressed God simply as "Father," and that Paul, with the Lord's Prayer in mind, speaks of the Spirit whereby we say "Abba, Father." But there is every reason to believe, as we have already seen, that Matthew has preserved the prayer in its authentic form. His additions to the version in Luke are all necessary, when we examine them, to the sequence of thought. The language he employs is purely Hebraic, as might be expected in the genuine utterance of Jesus. Above all, every word of the invocation, as Matthew gives it, is full of meaning. There is no amplifying of a simple phrase into a high-sounding one, as is commonly done in liturgies. Jesus was indeed averse to this practice, and the direct address "Father" might seem to be more consistent with his rule. But there is nothing superfluous in the longer invocation. It is as brief and condensed as Jesus could possibly make it if he was to express what was in his mind. God is high above us and yet cares for us as a Father, and he is our Father, who cares for us all alike.

We have here the typical instance of how Jesus transformed what he seemed to borrow. The name "Father" is used frequently in the Jewish prayers, but serves only to denote the privileged position of Israel. Men of other nations might pray to God but he would regard them as aliens; the people of Israel were his children. This idea of a special relation to God was based by the Rabbis on the emphatic statement in Exodus 4:22: "Thus saith the Lord, Israel is my son, my first-born, and I say unto thee, Let my son go that he may serve me, and if thou refuse to let him go I will slay thy son." Again and again in the Old Testament, as in the later literature, God is called Father, but always in this exclusive sense. The name is meant to suggest that for those outside of Israel God is not a Father, and that they cannot expect the mercy he will show to his own people. Jesus takes the familiar name and makes it express his protest against this narrow racial conception. When we call God our Father we address him simply as human beings. We lay aside all arrogant claims and come to him with the needs which are common to all men, asking him for that mercy which he bestows on all.

The name Father has been applied to God in many religions, but never with anything like the significance which it had for Jesus. Sometimes it has recalled a mythical story of how the tribe was literally descended from the god whom it worshipped. Sometimes it has been little more than a vague term of reverence. For the Greek thinkers it took on a philosophical meaning. Behind all things that exist there must be a first cause which we call God, and we may therefore speak of him as Father of the world of nature and of our own rational being. It may be possible to read something of this conception into the Lord's Prayer. Jesus never doubted that God had created the world, that he had breathed into men the spirit of life, that in their deeper instincts they have an affinity with him. But his whole interest was in the moral nature of God, who was not merely an abstract principle of Being or Reason or Law but a living Personality. There was a heart in him to which our own hearts could respond. He was righteous and compassionate. His will was one of infinite goodness. It was on this belief in God that the religion of Jesus was founded, and he expressed it in the opening words of his prayer.

He bade us, however, address God not only as "Our Father," but as "Our Father in heaven." This also is taken over from the Jewish prayers, where it answered to the old assumption that God was enthroned somewhere above the earth. It was customary to pray standing, with the hands outstretched and the eyes lifted towards the sky, where God was supposed to dwell. But already in the Jewish prayers the idea of God's throne in heaven carried with it the sense of his majesty and of the reverence due to him. As you prayed to him you were never to forget that he was far beyond your comprehension. He was in heaven and you were a creature of this earth. All this was in Jesus' mind, and also much more. It is evident from the petitions which follow that when he spoke of God as in heaven he sought to inspire us with perfect confidence in making our prayer. God is above this world and everything in it is subject to his will. We cannot doubt that whatever we ask of him he is able to do. He controls all these earthly forces which appear to hold us at their mercy, and we appeal to his sovereign power. And this Lord of all things is our Father, whose purpose is one of love.

The invocation thus prepares the way for the petitions, and again we must remind ourselves of their nature. They are not merely requests which we make to God but declarations of our faith in him. In the form of asking from God we assure him that we trust his wisdom and kindness and believe in the great end towards which he is working, in the world and in our own lives. It might seem as if the three first petitions might just as well have been plain affirmations. "God is holy." "His Kingdom is coming." "His will is certain to prevail." But for Jesus it is the very essence of prayer that we should seek to conform our own wills to that of God. Our desires may be all wrong, and we must make sure that what we ask for is not contrary to his nature and to his eternal plan. So when we pray we must seek first to know something of the mind of God. How does he himself act? What is the goal he has set before us? Unless we have this knowledge we are in the dark, and cannot tell what we should pray for. We may be wanting something to happen which will do us harm, some possession which will wreck our happiness, success in an undertaking which is morally wrong. So as we pray we must first seek clearness of vision, and this we can only gain by thinking of God and his high purposes. Those opening sentences of the prayer are true petitions. By means of them we ask God for illumination, for that knowledge of his will which will enable us to guide our own. The first thing necessary in a journey is to fix the direction in which you must go. You must know how the sun is moving before you can take a step yourself. So in prayer you must think first of God and frame all your wishes in accordance with his will.

The prayer begins, therefore, with the general petition "Let thy name be hallowed." You remind yourself that there is One who reigns supreme, to whom all created things must bow. This is clearly what the petition signifies, but it is expressed in language which has grown in some respects obscure. It was taken over by Jesus from the prayers to which he was accustomed, and reflects ideas which were peculiar to the religion of Israel. Why is it, for one thing, that such emphasis is laid on the divine Name? It is tempting to see a reference to the name "Father" which has just been used. Jesus has taught us to invoke God by this name, and might seem to impress on us in the first petition that it is the true name of God. But the Old Testament is full of allusions to God's holy name, and Jesus himself mentions it in a number of places where he is not speaking of God's Fatherhood. There can be little question that the name of God means simply God himself. It was assumed in ancient thought that the personality of a man was somehow bound up with his name, so that when you uttered his name the man himself was affected. This idea had such a hold on the Jewish mind that it was not permissible to speak the sacred name which God had communicated to Moses. It appears in the Bible as "Jehovah," but this only represents four consonants which are filled in by guess-work. The whole name was known only to the High-Priest, who uttered it

once a year when he stood before God in the holy of holies.
God himself was in his Name. For ancient thought the name
denoted not only a man's personality but all that it signified.
We still preserve this usage in such a phrase as "in the name
of the king," where the supreme authority is identified with
the name of him who wields it. So the name of God means
God in his divine office. He has many attributes but beneath them all is the fact that he is God and there is no
other. Our attitude to him must be one of absolute submis-
sion and awe.

The name of God is to be "made holy." This is a word
which meets us everywhere in the Bible, and which grows
in significance as we pass from earlier periods to later. The
idea at the root of it is that of separation. Men were conscious that over against the ordinary things of life there
were some that were of a different quality, and that these
had to be set apart and revered. Some objects possessed
mysterious powers. Some places had been the scene of marvellous things. Some experiences and states of mind were
unique, and could not be accounted for. Even in the most
primitive times men were feeling their way to the conviction
that they belonged to two separate worlds, and when they
came in contact with anything that suggested the higher one
they called it holy. At the outset the word carried no moral
import. A stone or a tree was holy if it was credited with
some magical efficacy; a man who saw visions or was subject
to fits of madness was a holy man. All that impressed the
primitive mind was the appearance amidst familiar things
of something that was inexplicable. Men had to reckon with
a power which was outside of the course of nature and yet
broke into it from time to time. There were things that were
holy, separate from this world, and they bore witness to God
who was the Holy One, apart from all that we can see or
comprehend.

For the Hebrews, almost from the beginning, the chief attribute of God was righteousness. It was this quality in Hebrew religion which marked it out from all others and made it capable of an endless development. There was much in its worship that was crude and repellent but it rested on the belief that God was righteous and that those who served him must obey the moral law. The word "holy" came thus to acquire an ethical meaning. God was holy, and everything that belonged to his worship—feast-days and altars and robes and candlesticks—partook of his holiness. But he was the righteous God, and all righteous acts were therefore of divine nature. A holy man was one who reflected in himself the justice and purity of God. But while holiness became another name for saintliness it still denoted a separation. God stands apart from the world, not only because he is high above it but because he is untouched by its sin and passion. Men share in his holiness in so far as they keep separate from all evil.

The first petition, then, is for the hallowing of God's name. Two ideas are here implied, both of which we meet constantly in the Old Testament and also in later Jewish thought. On the one hand, God himself hallows his name, makes manifest that he is apart from this world. The Old Testament is inspired throughout with the sense of the majesty of God, apparent in everything he has made and done. The heavens declare the glory of God. It speaks to us in all the works of nature, in the marvellous events which happened in ancient times and are happening still. "Holy, holy, holy is the Lord of hosts, the whole earth is full of his glory." God hallows his name. He reveals his glory everywhere; but men's eyes are so blinded that they cannot perceive it. This is the constant lament of the Old Testament prophets, and Jesus repeats it in many well-known sayings. He desires in his prayer that our dull senses may be made alive to the divine presence which is over the world and is ever manifesting itself.

On the other hand, God is hallowed through his people. This also is an idea which pervades the Old Testament. God had chosen Israel in order that this nation, dedicated to his service, should make him known to all the earth as the sovereign God. "Be ye holy for I am holy." This verse in Leviticus (19:2) was singled out by the later teachers as the very corner-stone of their religion. Israel was the people of God, who was the Holy One, separate from all evil, and Israel must keep itself apart, ordering its ways in all things by his commandments. The Jewish ritual was all intended to express this idea of a holy people, consecrated to the holy God. The Jewish ethic likewise had this as its central motive —to give effect in human action to the holiness of God. Other nations based their moral codes on tradition or social requirements or the natural instinct for what was right, Israel was guided by the one rule, "Ye shall not profane my holy name, for I will be hallowed among the children of Israel (Lev. 22:32). God was righteous, and the task of Israel was to represent him in all moral action, so that he might be known on earth as the holy God.

The Jewish ideal was mingled, no doubt, with much that was childish and superstitious. Not only the moral law but all the regulations about food and drink and observance of holy days were given a place in the hallowing of God's name. But the conception itself was a grand and uplifting one. Men were to live, not for this world, but for that to which they belonged in virtue of their higher nature. This is the fundamental idea of all religion and Jesus took it over and included it in his prayer. He expressed it in the traditional Jewish terms but gave it a new range of meaning. For one thing he no longer thought of one particular nation to which God had entrusted the hallowing of his name. All men were to feel that they were children of God, who desired them so to live that he might be known and honoured. Again, there is nothing in the prayer about special customs and ceremonies. The emphasis is all on moral obedience. Jesus was ever insisting that what God required of men was the practice of love and justice and mutual forgiveness. It was by this kind of service and no other that they would hallow his name. He is holy because he is absolutely good, and in so far as we have something in us of the divine goodness we show forth the nature of God. So the petition, in the last resort, is one of self-dedication. The aim of all noble souls is to forget the baser interests and look only to some higher end. The hero fights for the right, and cares nothing for what may happen to himself. The artist or thinker is worth little who puts his own reputation before his service to beauty or truth. It is the primary condition of all great work that it is done for God's honour and not for our own. This is the thought in that one passage of the Fourth Gospel which contains a clear echo of the Lord's Prayer. "Now is my soul troubled and what shall I say? Father, save me from this hour, but for this cause came I unto this hour. Father, glorify thy name" (John 12:27, 28). The motive of Jesus in all his actions was to fulfil the purpose of God, and for this he sacrificed all personal desires. So at the very beginning of his prayer he taught us to make the petition "Let thy name be hallowed." We pray as a community and as individual men and women, but must ever remember that it is not ourselves that matter. We ask God for all things needful in order that he may use us for his own ends. That is why life was given us, and if we feel otherwise we cannot rightly pray.

The petition that God's name may be hallowed is followed by that for the coming of his Kingdom, and the same sequence may be observed in Jewish prayers which must have been known to Jesus. The *Kaddish* begins, as we have seen, "Magnified and hallowed be thy great name, and let thy kingly rule be established in our life-time and in our day"; and the same connection of ideas is found in other prayers. It seems evident that Jesus has availed himself of the suggestion thus given him. He is conscious that the Kingdom cannot come until men have learned to acknowledge the holiness of God. We hear much in our time of a glorious future which will be brought about by increasing knowledge and new arrangements of the social system, and in these projects for a better world religion is left entirely out of sight. Sometimes, indeed, it is regarded as one of the ancient burdens from which we are struggling to get free. All this is the height of folly. We are reminded in the prayer of Jesus that religion must be the basis of all progress towards higher things. God's name must be hallowed. We must carry with us our reverence for God, who is enthroned above this world, or we have no goal before us and no inspiration to help us forward.

The petition for the Kingdom is the central one in the prayer. All of Jesus' teaching revolved around his conception of the Kingdom of God, the new order of things when God alone will reign. He told how everything would be transformed in the Kingdom and how men would themselves be different in their characters and wills. He bade them look forward to it and live for it even now. "Seek first the Kingdom of God and all other things will be added unto you." In this injunction he summed up his teaching, and all the petitions of his prayer converge in this one, "Thy Kingdom come." We have had occasion to note the variant to it which is found in Marcion's New Testament, "May thy holy Spirit come upon us and cleanse us." It dates back, apparently, to a very early time, and some scholars have argued that it preserves the genuine words of Jesus. But it cannot be accepted for many reasons, and chiefly because the whole prayer hinges on the petition for the Kingdom. There was a saying of one of the ancient Rabbis, "A prayer in which the Kingdom is never mentioned is no true prayer." The thought implied in this remarkable saying is a deep and far-reaching one. You cannot rightly pray unless you try to see your life in its larger setting. As you ask for help in your own struggle you must be mindful of the great cause of God, apart from which this little effort of yours is meaningless. Jesus would also have said that there must be some reference to the Kingdom in every prayer, but he would have gone much further. The hope of the Kingdom was for him the essential element in prayer. Whatever you ask for, it must be your chief desire that God should fulfil his purpose. "Seek first the Kingdom of God." When your heart is set on that you know what you ought to pray for; you have declared your ultimate desire and all the others fall into their place. So the Lord's Prayer all turns on this one petition for the Kingdom. We ask for daily bread that we may wait for the Kingdom; for God's forgiveness that we may be worthy to enter it; for power to resist temptation that we may never wander from the road that leads to it. The whole prayer is contained in the one petition.

The Kingdom is regarded as still to come, the object to which we aspire and which gives impulse to all our endeavour. In some of his sayings Jesus appears to think of it as already, in some degree, present, like a grain of mustard-seed which will grow into a spreading tree. More often, however, he expects, as in this prayer, that it will come in the future, all in a moment, when men are never looking for it. These two ideas do not contradict each other. The Psalmists can say, almost in the same breath, "The Lord reigneth" and "The Lord will reign." God has ever ruled the world and a time is coming when his power will be fully manifest. Jesus in like manner looks for a glorious consummation in the future, but calls on us to act here in the present as citizens of the Kingdom of God. But the prevailing idea in his teaching is that of a fulfilment which we have still to wait and pray for. In the Jewish prayers the emphasis is all on a speedy coming, "in our life-time, in our own days." There is nothing of this in the prayer of Jesus. The Kingdom is certain, but God will himself determine the time and manner of its coming, and we must live in hope. This hope, as Paul points out, is the grand incentive in our religion. In a sense it is more worth having than present possession. "For what a man seeth why does he yet hope for? But if we hope for what we see not, then do we in patience wait for it" (Rom. 8:25). But the idea in the prayer is not merely that in hope for the glorious future we shall bear up patiently, like prisoners who endure their dungeon by thinking of a day when they will be free. The hope of the future is to fill the present with a new significance. We are to feel that through all that is happening now God is working to bring in his Kingdom, and that we must work along with him. The prayer that the Kingdom should come is at the same time a prayer that God will help us to live for it now.

This is the thought which finds clear expression in the petition which follows, and which might seem to be the same one repeated in different words: "Thy will be done on earth as it is in heaven." In Luke's version of the prayer this petition is left out altogether, no doubt because it appeared merely to amplify the one before. This, however, was a mistaken view, for although the new petition is included in that for the Kingdom it has a necessary place of its own. For one thing it makes the prayer for the Kingdom urgent and practical. The consummation to which we look forward is still far distant, and while we believe in a perfect order which exists in heaven we may feel that here on earth we have nothing to do with it. Amidst the hard realities of life we often console ourselves with dreams of wealth and happiness, only to be thrown back, more dissatisfied than before, into the squalor and misery of the present. Men are apt to pray "Thy Kingdom come" in just this spirit. For a moment, as they utter the prayer, they have a glimpse of a blessed future when all things will be different; they are comforted with the thought of it. Then they remind themselves that they are now living on this earth and must be content with its standards. It cannot be expected of them that they should act in this imperfect world as if the Kingdom had come. But this, it is here impressed on us, is what we must try to do. The great principles of God's government are the same everywhere. We cannot conceive of any world in which truth and love and goodness are not the highest things. The earth we live in is under God's dominion, and we must do his will on earth as it is done in heaven.

Again, we are made to feel in this petition that while God is throned in heaven and we are earthly creatures whose life is but for a day, we yet have our part in his higher world. Among the things of time we must keep our hold on the everlasting, for it is the will of God which is ever fulfilling itself. Why is it that in our common lives we need always to be mindful of God? It might seem as if this were unnecessary, since our present interests stand by themselves and have nothing to do with ultimate mysteries. A man can find enough to do on his own little patch of land without ever troubling himself with how the earth was made or how it is related to the fixed stars. What can it matter to us in our every-day tasks whether God has a purpose or whether he exists at all? This is how many people reason, consciously or not, and Jesus would have us know that the will of God is a present reality. We have to reckon with it in everything we do, and unless we work along with it our labour is in vain. The Kingdom is in the future but it is not remote and imaginary. We must bring our passing lives into harmony with the eternal.

There are thus two sides to the petition. On the one hand we remind ourselves that God will assert his will, whatever may be the forces that oppose or hinder it. On the other hand we pray that we may obey his will, doing our little part to help it forward. We take our desires to God, remembering all the time that it is his will and not our own which will prevail. So what we really ask for is the willingness to submit ourselves to God. This was always the purpose of Jesus himself when he prayed. He did not seek to force his wishes on God but simply to know God's will that he might make it his. It has often been asked whether he joined on his own behalf in the prayer he taught his disciples and asked that his sins might be forgiven and that he might be saved from temptation. It cannot be doubted, however, that in its main purport the prayer came out of his own heart. We know that at Gethsemane, in the hour of his most intense personal need, he repeated this one petition of his prayer. "Father, all things are possible with thee. Take this cup from me. Nevertheless not what I will but what thou wilt."

The petition is one to which there is no real parallel in

the Jewish liturgies. There are indeed many allusions to God's will, and confessions that it is supreme in heaven and earth. But in all such passages the divine will is identified with the Law. Jesus thinks of it as the sovereign wisdom and justice and goodness by which all things are governed. Men are to recognise that behind all the confusions of this world God is working out his purpose. They can put their trust in him and seek, in all their action, to obey his will. This is the end and meaning of their life on earth. The petition thus unifies the prayer, connecting what goes before with all that follows. We first look upward and declare our faith in God who reigns in heaven. Our minds are uplifted with the thought of his majesty and his eternal purpose. Then we are reminded that this world also belongs to God. His purpose is fulfilling itself here and now, and he requires that in all our common action we should do his will. There is therefore no break between the two parts of the prayer. Its whole aim is to make us realise that our loftiest faith in God must have its outcome in our ordinary living, for the two things are not separate. The same will which rules in heaven can also be done here on earth.

So the prayer passes at once from sublime contemplation to the most elementary of human needs. "Give us to-day our daily bread." It has often appeared strange that Jesus should include in his prayer a petition which touches only on the material side of life, and many attempts have been made to interpret it symbolically or mystically. Does he not describe himself in John's Gospel as the bread of life, and must he not mean here that we should ever be growing in a life-giving fellowship with him? Or may there not be a hidden reference to sacramental bread, given us for our spiritual nourishment? Such explanations are unnatural on the face of them. The bread he bade us pray for was obviously that which we must have day by day to keep us alive. There is, however, this much truth in the mystical interpretations, that ordinary bread had for Jesus a sacred significance. He saw in it the visible sign that God cares for men as a father does for his children. They are to know, every time that bread is set before them, that they are dependent on God, without whose bounty they cannot live. Again and again in his teaching Jesus speaks of bread as the token of God's kindness, and of the kindness we must ourselves bestow on our fellow-men. At the Last Supper, when he wanted a symbol of his own great act of sacrifice, "he took bread and blessed it, giving thanks."

So when he taught us to pray for bread he was thinking of all that it signified. In providing us with bread God keeps us in life, and since our life is thus a continual gift from God we must use it worthily, in his service. Jesus never took the ascetic position that man, as a spiritual being, must despise the body and all its material demands. The very mark of a holy man in that age was to fast often and to keep aloof from society and reject all ordinary pleasure. Jesus "came eating and drinking" and participated in the common life. It was part of the splendid sanity of his religion that he allowed the material things their rightful place. He bade us pray for them, acknowledging that they came from God, who makes due provision for all his creatures. At the same time he warned us against their dangers. They fetter us to this world, and in the pursuit of them we lose sight of the true ends of life. God has placed us here in order that we may learn his will and work for his Kingdom, and the material things are necessary only in so far as they help us in this task. When they are valued for their own sake and our minds are wholly set on possessing them they become nothing but a hindrance.

It is in this light that we must understand the petition in the Lord's Prayer. We are to ask for bread, but only for that which is sufficient to sustain us while we pursue our higher task. In Luke the words are "Give us day by day," in Matthew, "Give us to-day." The idea is the same in both versions, but Matthew appears to be more original. The thought in Luke is general and colourless. We look at life as a whole and ask that on each day as it comes our portion may be dealt out to us. In Matthew this is made vivid and direct. We do not consider the future, which may never come, but only this day that is ours. We ask only for what we need to-day, bread enough to support us in doing this day's duties.

This brings us to the chief difficulty in the petition, perhaps in the whole prayer, and it is one that can never be definitely solved. In both versions there is reference to our "daily" bread, and the word employed (*epiousion*) is one which is found nowhere else in Greek literature, so that its exact meaning cannot be ascertained. Jesus must have used an Aramaic word which had no equivalent in Greek, and a new one was devised by translating it quite literally. As far back as we can go the church was puzzled by the word, and it is explained in different ways by the early Fathers. Some take it to mean "continual," the bread we constantly use. Others understand it as "necessary for existence." Others find a clue to it in a verse of Proverbs (31:8), "Give me neither poverty nor riches, but feed me with the bread which is sufficient for me." The trouble with all these interpretations is that they do not meet the requirements of Greek grammar. The word used in the prayer is one that should mean "belonging to to-morrow," and it cannot be rendered any other way without a twisting of ordinary rules. So if we take the word as it stands Jesus must have said "Give us this day our bread for to-morrow."

It may be argued that a petition of this kind would be contrary to Jesus' express teaching. He lays it down that we are not to be anxious for to-morrow, since to-morrow will take care of itself. He tells of the rich fool who was making ambitious plans when he heard a voice, "This night thy soul shall be required of thee." Jesus was ever insisting that we must serve God now and leave to-morrow in his hands. Perhaps this very petition was suggested by the story of the manna, which could be eaten only on the day it fell, and rotted if it was laid by for the next. Yet he uses a word which seems plainly to denote that the bread we pray for is that which we shall need to-morrow. It may be that he was thinking of a labouring man whose wage for one day was just enough to buy food for the day that followed. Or perhaps the Greek word for to-morrow is used in its literal sense of "the day coming on." You are to offer the prayer when the day is just beginning, and ask that in the course of it you will have your necessary bread. This, on the whole, is the likeliest interpretation, but however we understand the word the essential meaning is clear. The rendering "our daily bread" is an exceedingly happy one. It evades all the difficulties and yet expresses the thought which was certainly in Jesus' mind. He permits us to ask from God those things which are needful to our earthly life, but only for what will be sufficient for the passing day. For the unknown future we must trust ourselves to God.

This petition is followed immediately by that for forgiveness, and the sequence is no doubt intentional. To feel ourselves right with God is just as necessary as to be sustained in life, and we must ask for his forgiveness from day to day as we ask for our bread. This connection of the two petitions serves to explain what is meant by "trespasses." Jesus does not speak theologically of the sin inherent in man's nature, but only of definite acts which we know to be wrong. We are guilty of them continually and need every day to ask pardon for things that we did yesterday. Between Matthew's version and Luke's there are several differences which are more apparent than real. Matthew speaks of "debts," and Luke of "trespasses," but Luke is only translating a term which would be unintelligible to Gentiles. For Jews in the time of Jesus God was the great Creditor to whom all our service is due, and his forgiveness is the generous remission of a debt. Jesus makes use of this idea in his parable of the man who owed ten thousand talents. The original words of the prayer were doubtless "Forgive us our debts," but Luke explains their meaning. Another difference is that Matthew has the past tense, "as we have forgiven," where Luke has the present, suggesting that in the very act of praying for our own forgiveness we freely forgive our fellow-men. This was probably the thought of Jesus. In prayer to God you are to be filled with the sense of his divine compassion, so that there will be no room in your mind for petty animosities against your neighbours. But if this was Jesus' meaning it is conveyed just as well in Matthew's version, translated as it is from Aramaic, which was apt to make little distinction between a present tense and a past.

There is a third and more important difference. According to Matthew Jesus said "Forgive us as we forgive others," while in Luke we have "Forgive us, for we also forgive." The effect is to make God's forgiveness conditional on our own. We approach him conscious that we have done our part, and expect him in return to grant us pardon. Now it is true that Jesus told us, "With what measure you mete it will be measured unto you." Ever and again he points to an inexorable law by which our actions recoil on us and we receive from life just the good or evil we have worked for. He speaks of the Kingdom itself as a reward, only bestowed on those who have proved worthy. But prayer, by its very nature, is an appeal to the generosity of God, and this note has never been struck so unmistakably as in the Lord's Prayer. We are to throw ourselves on God because he is our Father, who will give us out of his free goodness far more than we have deserved. To make his forgiveness conditional on what we have done ourselves is to bring Jesus' prayer to the level of that of the self-righteous Pharisee whom he condemned.

The idea that we must ourselves forgive if we would be forgiven is entirely absent from the Jewish prayers. They are full of pleas for forgiveness, accompanied with cries of repentance and appeals to God's mercy, but nothing is said of the mercy we must show to one another. For Jesus, and this was one of the new elements in his religion, the two things were inseparable. It is often assumed that the second clause of the petition is only a kind of after-thought. What we pray for is to be forgiven our trespasses, and the sentence might have stopped there, but the reflection is thrown in that we ought ourselves to be kind to those who have offended us. This, however, is an integral part of the petition, indeed the vital part. What we really pray for is to have in us the forgiving spirit, for without that we cannot hope for the forgiveness of God. Perhaps the best commentary on this part of the Lord's Prayer is Shakespeare's great passage on mercy, which is directly inspired by it, as is evident from the closing lines:

> We do pray for mercy,
> And that same prayer doth teach us all to render
> The deeds of mercy.

The poet has observed that the two parts of the petition

must be taken together. Praying to God for mercy we are also praying that we may ourselves be merciful.

Jesus has himself indicated in other places of his teaching why he combines the two ideas. He tells, for instance, that when a man has laid his gift on the altar and suddenly remembers that he has a quarrel with his neighbour, he must leave his offering incomplete and go first to be reconciled with his brother-man. Until then he cannot approach God, for there is no correspondence between himself and God, whose nature is one of mercy. So long as there is nothing in common between ourselves and God we cannot hold fellowship with him in prayer. We must forgive in order to be forgiven, not because God repays us what we have earned, but because our wills must be in harmony with his own will. While we cherish our small resentments there is a barrier between ourselves and him, and it must be broken down. Forgive those who have injured you, and you can speak to God in a language he will understand.

It has sometimes been remarked as a grave defect in the Lord's prayer that nothing is said in it of those social duties with which the rest of his teaching is so largely concerned. He made the prayer for the use of his community and ought surely to have reminded it that it stood for a new kind of fellowship in which all men should love and serve one another. Yet this whole side of the Christian message is apparently lost sight of in the great Christian prayer. This, however, is not so. All that Jesus teaches elsewhere of how we should act towards others is summed up and brought to a point in these few words, "as we forgive those who trespass against us." At the root of all our social problems lies the one sad fact that men are unforgiving. They return evil for evil, and small injuries give rise to greater ones, ever more complicated. We devise laws and institutions to put things

right, and dream of a society in which all will understand
and help each other. But no system will ever enable men
to live happily together if there is no spirit of mutual for-
bearance. We all have our shortcomings, and yours do in-
jury to your neighbour and his to you, and while we keep
retaliating there will always be strife and misery. If men
could only agree, even for a day or two, to forgive one another, almost all our social difficulties would disappear. And
this will never be possible until we are so possessed with the
sense of God's mercy to us that we shall be willing ourselves
to be merciful.

We pray that past offences may be forgiven, and in the
next petition we pray that we may not repeat them or fall
into new ones. The idea springs up easily in most religions
that since there are means of winning back God's favour we
need not trouble too much about our sins. To be sure, you
have done something wrong, and may do it again, but the
way out is always open. You have only to ask God to forgive
you and he will do so. "He's a good fellow and 'twill all be
well." Jesus seeks to impress on us that God's mercy is
granted in order that we may break away from evil-doing.
"Forgive us our trespasses" must also mean "Lead us not
into temptation."

The words of this petition would be familiar to those who
first listened to Jesus. Two prayers, one for the morning and
one for the evening, were repeated every day by pious Jews,
and they both contained the words "Bring us not into the
hand," that is, into the power or influence "of any temptation." The Jewish parallel is here of real value for the understanding of the Lord's Prayer. We pray to be guarded from
"temptation," and this word in Greek means simply "trial"
and can be applied to anything that tests our strength or

endurance. It can be used in a moral sense of an allurement
to do evil, but also of any experience which is hard to bear.
A severe illness, a bereavement, a crisis in business, a struggle of any kind is a "trial" to which we may prove unequal.
So it has been held that Jesus had this wider meaning in his
mind, and taught us to pray that God should spare us from
all troubles that might over-tax our strength. This is indeed
the substance of most of our prayers, and Jesus may well
have thought of trial generally. But it seems clear that in the
Jewish parallels the word had reference to moral evil, and
we can infer from the previous petition that it has this meaning also in the prayer of Jesus. He had spoken of "trespasses,"
and his mind is still moving on those lines.

The Jewish prayers also throw a light on the outstanding
difficulty of this petition. It seems to assume that God is
himself the author of temptation. We are to ask him not to
lead us into it, as if he were purposely exposing us to the
seductions of evil. We cannot but feel that such an idea is
contrary to the thought of Jesus. His ministry began with
a temptation, but he never doubted that it was Satan who
tempted him. He was tempted at Cæsarea Philippi, when
Peter urged him to avoid suffering and death, and there too
he said "Get thee behind me, Satan." He took for granted
always that attraction to evil must come from a power hostile
to God. It has been pointed out by some recent scholars that
in Aramaic the imperative can be used in a "permissive"
sense, that is, you may say "Do not break that cup" when
you mean "Do not let it be broken." Thus when Jesus said
"Lead us not" he would only imply "Do not allow us to be
led." This is very likely the true interpretation, but it does
not wholly remove the difficulty. If temptation comes to us
by God's permission he may fairly be said to cause it. When
you do nothing to stop a man who is walking towards a
precipice you are responsible for his fall.

The difficulty was recognised from the earliest times, as we may gather from a passage in the Epistle of James, addressed, most probably, to people who used this petition as an excuse for their moral weakness. "Let no man say when he is tempted, I am tempted by God; for God cannot be tempted with evil, neither tempts he any man. But every man is tempted when he is drawn away by his own lusts and enticed" (James 1:13, 14). It is admitted, however, in the same passage, that there is truth in the other view. "Blessed is the man who endureth temptation, for when he is tried he shall receive the crown of life." Temptation is here regarded as the means ordained by God for the discovery and the perfecting of his true servants. This is a thought which meets us frequently in the Old Testament. Israel was tempted in the wilderness and fell. God tempted Abraham and found him faithful. The Psalmist prays, "Search me and try me and see if there is any evil way in me." It is one of the cardinal ideas of the Old Testament that life is a process of trial, and that God has willed it so.

The petition may thus be taken in its literal sense. Jesus acknowledges that God himself allows us to be tempted, and bids us pray that we may be spared the test. His object throughout the prayer is to reconcile us to the will of God, and it might seem strange that in this one instance he would have us try to escape from it, but there is no suggestion of resisting the divine will. The idea is rather that we must not presume too much on our own strength. Temptation is never so dangerous as when you feel confident that it cannot overcome you, that while others may have fallen you are made differently and will be able to stand. Jesus warns us that we cannot trust ourselves. We must pray God to save us from any trial in which we may miserably fail. So we are reminded here again of Jesus' own attitude in face of the dreadful ordeal which had not yet become inevitable. "Father, if it be possible let this cup pass from me." We have all the right to pray in the same manner. "May we escape the trial if we may; be pleased to lead us by some other road; but if there is no other, thy will be done."

Much in the petition may be explained from the Jewish prayers which were almost certainly in Jesus' mind. "Lead us not into the power of any temptation," that is, into circumstances in which temptation may prove too strong for us. There may not be anything inherently wrong in them, and they may even offer us a grand opportunity. A man wishes, for instance, to have a post of high authority, or one which gives him control of large sums of money. He feels sure that in this position he will do splendid service, but too often when he has gained it he finds his downfall. He has ventured within the power of temptation, and does not have the strength to resist it. A wise man will be distrustful of himself. He will not grasp at every chance that entices him but will rather pray that he may not be led into any situation which may demand too much of him. God may compel him at times to accept a heavy responsibility, and with God's help he will bear it manfully. But he knows his weaknesses and limitations and will avoid the danger if he may.

The word "temptation" has come to be applied in a narrow sense to inducements that appeal to the lower passions —greed, self-interest, sensuality—but there are many temptations which attack our higher nature, and it was these, perhaps, which Jesus had chiefly in mind. A bereavement or a great misfortune causes you to lose faith in God. When you have laboured hard for the good of others and meet only with ingratitude you become scornful of your fellow-men. The intellectual man comes to trust wholly in knowledge.

The industrious man is so absorbed in practical duties that he forgets his soul. The man of spiritual nature is careless of the world around him. There is no human activity which does not bring with it its special temptation, and Jesus was aware of this when he framed the petition. It was not meant only for people of weak will or prone to the enticements of the flesh, but for all men and women, whatever may be their occupations, or the character of their lives. We are always to be watchful, conscious that every path in life has its moral dangers, against which we must be on our guard. We are to ask God so to lead us that we may serve him faithfully in any state to which he calls us and yet escape the temptation which it is sure to entail.

The last petition of the prayer is closely connected with the previous one, so much so that it may seem merely to repeat it. This is no doubt the reason why in Luke's version it disappears. Yet it is a new and separate petition, which is necessary to complete the other. We have prayed not to fall into temptation, but what if we have already fallen? All men are conscious that they have done so, and that even at the present moment they are in the toils of some grievous evil. By their own strength they cannot free themselves and must pray to God that he will deliver them. The last petition, so far from being superfluous, may be regarded as the emphatic one, which is therefore reserved for the close. We pray to God because there is evil within us and all around us, and we can do nothing without his help.

The petition is thus wider in its range than the one before. It takes account, not only of moral danger, but of every kind of peril and distress. Jesus thought, however, of physical evils in their moral aspect. Life, as he conceived it, is given us for the service of God, and the effect of sickness, poverty, disaster, oppression is to crush the spirit and hinder us in our task. We hear much in the Gospels of Jesus' acts of healing, and they are accompanied in almost every case with some word of warning or encouragement. He makes it clear that he has struck off certain fetters in order that the sufferer may live henceforth to better purpose. Every man or woman was for him a child of God, destined to noble service, and he was impatient of anything that disabled. He wanted men to be free, and made it a main part of his ministry to remove their burdens, physical and social as well as spiritual. So in his prayer he bids us ask God to deliver us from all evil.

We come here to the peculiar difficulty of this petition. The Greek word employed may be taken either as abstract or personal, "from evil" or "from the evil one"; and either translation may be right. Jesus may have spoken in general terms of evil, or have made his thought more forcible by naming Satan as the author of evil. In his teaching elsewhere he expresses himself in both ways. He declares that outward purity is of no avail since all wicked actions "proceed out of the heart of man." But he also ascribes them to the prompting of Satan. He makes him the cause even of bodily ills, as when he says of the paralytic woman, "Satan hath bound her these thirty years." The same variation is found in the Jewish literature of the time. Satan is regarded as the source of evil, but it is also attributed to "the wicked principle," inherent in man's own nature. It is not possible to say definitely how the word in the prayer should be understood, especially as we have it only in the Greek form and cannot tell what it was in Jesus' own language. Most likely, however, he spoke abstractly of "evil." In the previous petition he had certainly said "temptation," not "the tempter" and there was no reason why his thought should now take a different turn. It has been pointed out, too, that in the Jewish literature Satan is never described allusively as "the evil one," and Jesus would not go out of his way to invent the title. The prayer, in every word of it, is direct and natural, and we cannot suppose that it closed with an artificial term. Whatever may have been the word he used Jesus was thinking of "evil," and we may assume that this was what he said.

The final Doxology was not originally a part of the prayer. It does not appear in any of the older manuscripts, and seems to have been unknown to most of the early Fathers. When it was introduced we cannot tell, but it seems to have been commonly used in the second century, for the author of the Didachê includes it, as a matter of course, in his quotation of the prayer. There can be little question that it was added by the church, in conformity with the practice, taken over from Judaism, of closing all public prayers with a solemn ascription of praise to God. An addition of this kind would be made the more readily as the prayer would otherwise have ended with the word "evil." It may be noted that the Doxology helps to confirm the authenticity of the prayer. The church cannot itself have made the prayer for use in its worship, for it was found to be unsuitable for this purpose. Before it could be adopted into the church service this closing Doxology had to be added.

It is derived from the farewell prayer of David in the first book of Chronicles (29:11). "Thine O Lord is the greatness and the power and the glory and the victory and the majesty. Thine is the Kingdom, O Lord, and thou art exalted as head above all." These words are echoed in one of the later Psalms. "They shall speak of the glory of thy Kingdom and talk of thy power; thy Kingdom is an everlasting Kingdom" (Ps. 145:11, 12). The little hymn of praise had probably been long in use in the services of the Temple and the synagogue, and had found its way into Christian worship long before it was incorporated in the Lord's Prayer. It was modified, however, under the influence of the prayer itself, which centred in the petition for the Kingdom, and rested on the confidence that God is all-powerful and that his name is hallowed. The ancient Doxology is brought into harmony with the prayer, and completes it in noble words.

It was customary in later Judaism to add the words "for ever" (literally "for the ages") to every ascription of praise to God. This was done, we are told, by way of protest against the heresy which denied any future world. True worshippers were to remember always that God reigns eternally and that no changes can affect his purpose. This "for ever" is set like a seal on the Doxology, and here again we are taken back to the prayer itself. "Thy will be done on earth as it is in heaven." The God whom we worship now will be sovereign in all ages and all worlds.

"Amen" was the Hebrew word for certainty, and was used to express a full assent to a statement made. Hence it became the response of an assembly to a prayer made on behalf of all. The actual speaker was only a mouth-piece and his words had weight only when the others confirmed them with the Amen. There is no evidence that Jesus himself added this term of assent to his prayer. He indeed meant it to be offered by a community, but was thinking all the time of individuals, who would repeat it in their inner chamber. All the response he asked of them was that of their personal faith. At a later time the recitation of the prayer was a stated act of public worship, and each one in the company made it his own by joining in the Amen.

CHAPTER VI

THE IMPLICATIONS OF THE PRAYER

Two things in our religion have come to us directly from Jesus himself—the Lord's Supper and the Lord's Prayer. His teaching was all informal, and he never tried, like the founders of other religions, to bind his followers for ever to some fixed system of creed and practice. He left them free to think for themselves and to throw his message into new forms which would keep its meaning fresh and real in every changing time. Yet he bequeathed to them these two ordinances which they were to preserve just as they had come from his hands—the Supper which tells what he did for us, and the Prayer which sums up what he taught us.

These two acts of worship have a place by themselves in our religion, and are like the two poles on which it turns. A Christian service would be complete if it consisted only of an observance of the Supper and a repetition of the Lord's Prayer. Between them they represent everything that we believe, and they are necessary to each other. We cannot rightly say the prayer without remembering the Cross, and we cannot celebrate the Supper unless we mean to follow the way of Jesus in our daily lives. In all times men have been conscious that in these two gifts Jesus gave us every-thing, and the chief aim of Christian thought has been to discover the full significance of the Lord's Supper and the Lord's Prayer.

The Supper in itself is a very simple rite, nothing but an ordinary meal which Jesus turned to a high and holy pur-pose; and the Prayer is of a similar character. It consists of a few plain sentences, and is taken over, for the most part, from prayers already familiar to everybody. Here, too, it might be said "He took bread and blessed it." He laid hold of the common substance of prayer and transformed it into the utterance of man's deepest faith and longing. There have been many, from the earliest times, who have seen little that was remarkable in the prayer. They have gone over it, sen-tence by sentence, and have pointed to passages in Jewish and heathen prayers where the same thing was said in much the same words. But they have failed to observe that out of the old material Jesus has made something new. His prayer is far more than the sum of its parts. It is pervaded by a new sense of God and of man's relation to God and of the meaning of human life. When we utter the prayer with full sincerity it is this new element in it of which we are chiefly aware. It is the perfect expression not only of certain needs but of the religious spirit. Men have responded to it, and will ever continue to do so, because it speaks to them of the ultimate truths they are meant to live by.

Carlyle has told, in a letter written shortly before he died, that during a sleepless night he had set himself to think out the Lord's Prayer, and had found that at every point he was carried beyond his depth. He felt that he might explore it for ever without fully knowing what was involved in any one of those simple petitions he had learned as a child. This was early realised by Christian teachers, and they made it their task to discover the hidden import of the Lord's Prayer. Their interpretations of it were often beautiful and suggestive but we can now see that they set out from a wrong assumption. They believed that since his words were all so simple Jesus must have meant something different from what he said. He had spoken to all appearance of common things, but must have been thinking of doctrines and mysteries. The prayer, as they understood it, was a kind of allegory, every word of which was fraught with a hidden significance. But it is certain that this was not the intention of Jesus. He expressly taught that in their approach to God men should say plainly what was in their hearts, and he gave his prayer as an example of how this should be done. If he had wrapped it in a veiled language he would have broken his own explicit rule. The old expositors were mistaken in their method, but they were right in their belief that much more is implied in the prayer than is actually said. With all its simplicity it contains, at least in outline, all that was profoundest in later Christian thought.

Dante, in the 9th canto of his Purgatory, has paraphrased the prayer as it was generally explained in the theology of his time. The passage is worth quoting as the finest example of that old manner of exposition which is sometimes followed still.

> Our Father, thou who dwellest in the heaven,
> Not circumscribed, but for the greater love
> Thou bearest to the first effects on high.
> Praised be thy name and thy omnipotence
> By every creature, as befitting is
> To render thanks to thy sweet effluence.
> Come unto us the power of thy dominion.
> For unto it we cannot lift ourselves,
> If it come not, with all our intellect.

Even as thy angels make a sacrifice
Of their own wills to thee, Hosanna singing,
So may all men make sacrifice of theirs.
Give unto us this day our daily manna,
For, wanting it, in this rough wilderness,
Backward goes he who tries most to advance.
And even as we the trespass we have suffered
Pardon in one another, pardon thou
Benignly, and regard not our desert.
Our virtue which is easily overcome
Put not to proof with the old Adversary,
Save us from him who presses us so hard.

(Longfellow's translation)

Dante takes each sentence of the prayer and brings it into line with mediæval doctrine. God is the Father in the sense that all other being has proceeded from him in a descending scale. Men must lay aside all pride of intellect and passively receive what God has given. They must give up their individual wills, offering them to God by way of a sacrifice. Divine grace is imparted daily through the sacraments, and without it there can be no true life. God and Satan are ever contending for the possession of men's souls. Dante has indeed realised the power and magnificence of the prayer, but he has done so in spite of his theology. With the insight of a great poet and a man of deep religious spirit he has entered into the mind of Jesus. The prayer has spoken to him for itself, and ever and again, while seeking to interpret it, he falls back on its own words, aware that he can put nothing into them which they do not already contain. Yet the prayer, in his version of it, has become different. The doctrinal ideas which he expresses, are not those of Jesus.

It is by another road than the old allegorical one that we

must find our way to the profounder import of the prayer. There is indeed philosophy in it, and also mysticism and doctrine, but they are not to be found by forcing into it symbolical meanings which are not there. Every sentence must be taken as it stands. God cares for us as a father does for his children. He rules in heaven, but we can do his will on earth. He gives us the bread we live by, pardons our offences, gives us power to resist temptation and escape from evil. The greatness of the prayer consists just in this, that it takes the common facts of life and makes us conscious of all that they signify. In ancient times when men sought to explain the wonders of the natural world they turned away from them and devised beautiful myths of how beings of a higher order were transformed into the mere material things we see. The geologist to-day lifts a stone which is lying at his feet; he knows that the mystery is here. If he can only read the evidence of this stone by the roadside he will reach back to all that happened when the mountains and oceans were forming. It is in a similar manner that Jesus explains the ways of God. He bids us look at the familiar things just as they are, and try to understand them. He uses no symbolic language, for the facts themselves have a significance far deeper than we can ever fathom. We must try to realise this, as he himself did, when we say his prayer.

It is from this point of view that we discern the larger conceptions which were in his mind. While he spoke of ordinary things he was thinking of all that was involved in them. How have we come by our daily bread? Why should we forgive injuries and resist temptation? How do we get the power to do so? Our life, which seems so ordinary, has a meaning in it which is far beyond our comprehension, and in everything we do we come in contact with the final realities. So in his prayer Jesus is not speaking in riddles. He is trying, rather, to lift the veil which prevents us from seeing what is right before our eyes.

For one thing he makes us feel, in every sentence of the prayer, that our life in time is bound up with the eternal. We find ourselves on this earth, busied with its little passing interests, but have our place appointed us in God's great order of things. If we are to live truly we must take account of that eternal world to which we belong, and keep ourselves in harmony with it. In some dim fashion this truth has been apparent to men ever since they began to think. A traveller has told that in a remote valley in central Asia he came on a forgotten tribe which apparently had never learned a religion; but he observed that the old woman in whose hut he had found refuge used every morning, when she went out to her work, to bow herself to the rising sun, and when she returned in the evening she stood for a moment and bowed to the setting sun. May we not say that this was indeed religion, in its bare essence? It was the recognition that man's life is part of a greater one, that he accomplishes his daily task in company with a power which is above him and yet in some way related to himself. This conviction is rooted in the very nature of man and marks the difference between him and the beasts that perish.

Men have always been aware that they have part in the eternal world and must conform their lives to it. They have felt, too, that they could do so only by obeying certain moral laws. It is true that their religion has often been associated with cruel and perverted beliefs. The Roman poet declared, and the charge has often been repeated, that religion has been the cause of much of the world's evil. There is truth in the accusation, but it could never have been made unless men had felt instinctively that religion ought always to stand for what is right. The eternal power of which we are conscious must be one of justice and goodness, and you offend against it whenever you do wrong. An idea of this kind is clearly present in all religions, however barbarous. Religion has its very root in the assurance that from this world's ills and oppressions we can appeal to the goodness of God.

Our life on earth is bound up with the eternal; God who is in heaven is our Father. This was a truth of which men had always been dimly conscious, though before Jesus it had never been fully realised. But in the Lord's Prayer it is combined with another, which he had apprehended for the first time. Since our earthly life is linked up with that of God everything in it must be of endless value. Much has been said in all ages of the unreality of life. It comes and goes like a dream, and all those passions and interests which once stirred us so deeply seem, when we look back on them, so unmeaning. "What shadows we are and what shadows we pursue"; so said a great statesman when his rival suddenly died in the middle of a fierce debate. The same reflection has forced itself at times on all of us. In the midst of life we are in death, which is always beside us, mocking at all our hopes and efforts. But there is another truth, which stands out clearly in the Lord's Prayer. Life is not an illusion but is infinitely more real than we ever know. In the midst of life we are in eternity. We seem to be shadows chasing shadows but all the time we are face to face with the great realities. They are present to us in all our common experience and if we could rightly see these passing things they would enable us to know God and to work along with him in the fulfilment of his purpose. His will may be done on earth as it is in heaven.

It was thus the aim of Jesus to bring home to us the tremendous reality of life. He was never obsessed, as other teachers have been, with the grim fact of death, and there is no mention of it in his prayer. This may well appear strange, for the whole object of religion, as many people conceive it, is to prepare us for death and the hereafter. But Jesus did not speak of death, for to his mind the great mystery was life. He was confident that when it ended God had some fuller life in store for his children, but all this he was content to leave in God's hands. Whatever the new life might be it would only continue and perfect that which we have now, for here on earth we have fellowship with God. In the one passage in which he speaks explicitly of immortality Jesus grounds his faith in this, that we have entered on it already. "He is not the God of the dead but of the living, for all live unto him." As children of God, men belong to the eternal world, and death cannot touch their essential being. The Lord's Prayer gives utterance to this conviction. It is concerned with the present life, which we accept as a matter of course because we are blind to the wonder of it. Jesus tries to make us see it as it really is. Our life in time is also in eternity, and we must live it with that truth in mind. Our needs are manifold and we must bring them before God in prayer, but our chief need is to know God's presence with us now, and so order our earthly life that we may live unto him.

It is in this light that we must understand the prayer. We can see, for one thing, why it is occupied with matters of every day. This has often been singled out as its chief defect, that it moves on too low a level and symbolic meanings have to be read into it to make it more spiritual. It is indeed natural to pray to God on high occasions, when faced with death or disaster, when called on to make great decisions, when rapt in a mood of devotion; but why trouble him about little things which pass and are forgotten? Even the Pagan moralists were aware that the mere accidents of life were of no account, but Jesus appears to magnify them and to degrade the whole idea of prayer by connecting it with trivial things. But it was just this Pagan attitude to prayer which he sought to change. For him there was nothing in man's experience that was trivial. There could not be, for the earthly life, as he saw it, was woven in with eternal things. Each event that goes by unnoticed is fraught with endless possibilities. Everything you do or suffer in this mysterious life is like a seed thrown into the ground, which may grow into a tree or a mighty forest. We are dealing always, not with things we can weigh and measure, but with incalculable forces, and what seems little in our eyes may have consequences that will never cease. It was the aim of Jesus to make us feel the significance of all our common actions. We are to remember always that we are living in eternity as well as in time, and that infinite issues are involved in everything we do. That is the very reason why we pray. If all the factors in life had their known value, as in a game of chess, we could depend on our own skill and prudence. Countless people have lived on that assumption, and have often attained to high prosperity without asking any help from God. But sooner or later they have found themselves betrayed by their self-confidence. Life does not consist wholly in moving set pieces on a board. In all our actions we are working among things beyond our knowledge. We are causing influences to flow in from another world, which we cannot control and which will override our most careful plans. So we ask God to guide us, for we walk blindly by ourselves. Jesus, in his prayer, takes the common things of life and brings them into relation to God and his eternal purpose. "Our Father who art in heaven—give us this day our daily bread."

In the mere struggle to exist from day to day we are in contact with the highest. We are learning to know God and put our trust in him.

Again, this prayer, in which men wait on God as his children, awakens in us the sense of our human personality. All religions hitherto had been collective. Each city or nation had its god who was supposed to hold it under his protection, caring for individuals only as members of the favoured community. This is the idea which pervades the Old Testament and which is implied in the name "Father" as it was used in the Jewish prayers. By means of it the individual declared that although he was nothing in himself he was yet one of the nation which God had chosen. It was the grand discovery of Jesus that every human being had a destiny of his own, a personal claim on God. This may be regarded as the distinctive element in the religion of Jesus. His conceptions of God's power and wisdom and goodness had all, in some measure, been anticipated, but he was the first who dared to believe that the sovereign God was mindful of every human soul. He taught us to call God "Father" in the consciousness that each one of us has something in him of God's own nature, and that his life, though it may count for little by earthly standards, has a value in God's sight.

The thought of God's providence was ever present to Jesus and finds expression in many a beautiful saying and parable. It underlies the Lord's Prayer and gives it meaning. We are to pray to God in the confidence that he knows us one by one and will give to us what we separately need. The petitions are all so framed that every one can apply them to himself at this particular moment. All men are subject to hunger and sin and temptation and distress, and we speak of God of our common human needs. But we all feel them differently, and as we make the general prayer we think of our individual difficulties and temptations, assured that God takes knowledge of us and will guide us in our own lives.

Not only so, but while we trust God's providence we seek a personal fellowship with him. The old attempts to explain the prayer mystically were mistaken, but there was a genuine insight at the heart of them. In its deeper implications the prayer is profoundly mystical. It leads back, at every point, to the conviction that God who rules the world is also within us, and that we can hold an inner communion with him. The Fourth Evangelist is often accused of reading his own mystical ideas into the practical teaching of Jesus. Where in the other Gospels, it is asked, do we hear of a new birth or a union with God through Christ? The answer is that this is the ultimate message of all the Gospels. Jesus was ever teaching that God is close to us, that our will must be one with God's will, that our own hearts bear witness that we are children of God. These are the truths implicit in the Lord's Prayer. It deals with the needs and trials of our ordinary life, but we pray for God's help in them because we feel that he is present with us, that he knows us personally. Through all these earthly experiences he is bringing us into union with himself.

But while the prayer is intensely personal it is also communal. Jesus meant it to be prayed in unison by his company of disciples, who would thus assure themselves that the faith of each one of them was the faith of all. But while the prayer is communal there is nothing in it that is sectarian. It contains no hint of any peculiar customs or doctrines or forms of worship. This, it may be noted, is one of the strongest proofs that it did not originate in the later church, which never forgot that it was an elect society in the midst of a hostile world. The Lord's Prayer is universal. It is concerned wholly with needs which are common to all humanity. Jesus saw men divided, and it was plainly his object, when he made the prayer, to unite them in one brotherhood.

How this may be done has ever been the great problem which all our laws and institutions were intended to solve. In our time it has become more terribly urgent than in any previous age. It is no longer possible to keep each group apart and make it united within itself. Distances have been broken down, and all races, in spite of themselves, are thrown together. Social partitions are likewise disappearing, and men are everywhere plunging madly forward, like an army in rout or an assembly startled by the cry of fire. How can order be restored in this confusion? How can men be brought to realise that they are all one family and that the good of each is the good of all? We indeed hear much of the brotherhood of man, but the proofs of it commonly put forward seem all to point the other way. The passions and appetites which we have in common are shared by the animals. We have the gift of reason but it is bestowed in endless degrees, from the mind of the savage to that of Shakespeare or Newton. Neither can we say that we are bound together by material interests, for it is just here that we are always clashing. Any unity that is achieved among these lines is sure to prove deceptive. If the race of man is to survive on earth it must make itself one; this is growing more and more apparent every day. But where is the bond which will hold it together?

Jesus found it in that element of man's nature which makes him man. Living in this world he also belongs to another. He is never so much identified with earthly things but he looks beyond them. He is able to renounce them and to sacrifice this life altogether for a hope or ideal which will never have any visible fulfilment. The ultimate springs of his action are spiritual, for essentially he is a spiritual and not an earthly being. Men have always had this sense that here they are strangers, and it is this, in the last resort, that brings them into fellowship. They are like people of one land who are sojourning in another but only feel at home in the society of their countrymen, with whom they can speak their native language and exchange old memories and affections. The prayer of Jesus appeals to that sympathy which men feel with one another in a world which is not truly their own. It speaks of our Father, of the will that is done in heaven, of the higher life to which we are aspiring amidst earthly hardships and temptations. All men respond to the prayer because it touches those instincts and longings which lie deepest in their human nature, and by teaching them to say this prayer together Jesus seeks to unite them. Most of our discords arise simply from this, that we have no real knowledge of one another. We mingle in all kinds of superficial relations but each one keeps his inner thoughts and motives to himself. You may live for years in constant intercourse with another man, only to find at the end that you have never known him nor has he known you. So Jesus gave his prayer, not only to be spoken to God in the inner chamber, but to be repeated by companies of men. Each one thus reveals himself to the others, and they all discover that in their vital interests they are at one. It is only in this way that men will ever be truly united. They must learn that the things which divide them are only on the surface and may soon be adjusted with a little patience and good-will. In their central needs and in the ends towards which they are striving they are all the children of one Father. If the distracted world is ever to find itself in harmony it will not be through science or culture or organisation but through a deeper understanding of the Lord's Prayer.

The feeling of many people when they look on the sea for the first time is one of disappointment. They had expected an illimitable space to be unrolled before them, and all that meets the eye is a strip of water, no wider, to all appearance, than their inland lakes. In the same manner there are those who are disappointed with the Lord's Prayer. It has been treasured through all these centuries by countless millions of Christians as the grand charter of their religion, but there seems to be little in it that makes it different from other prayers. It covers only a few of the manifold needs of men; it touches on nothing that has not always been apparent. But the ocean extends far beyond our vision to the ends of the earth, and this prayer of Jesus likewise stretches out into the infinite. All the world of truth that lies behind it is part of the prayer itself.

It is the most comprehensive of all prayers, and besides all else it is the Lord's Prayer. This is the ultimate secret of its appeal. It has come to us directly from Jesus himself, and while he fell back on familiar words he transmuted them by making them his own. As we repeat his prayer we make contact with the Lord. We remember how he lived and died and what he taught us. There is not a word in it which does not recall some act of his or some immortal saying. Not only so, but through his prayer he communicates something of his spirit. We learn from it to think as he did about God, and the meaning of human life. It is indeed the universal prayer, and men of all religions and all modes of thought can join together in offering it. Yet it is the Christian prayer, and only those who believe in Christ can pray it rightly. For he put himself into his prayer, and what we seek from it is not merely an answer to our petitions but a living fellowship with Christ.

A.M.

Tu

We V6 Ps. 144 BE 742 BD 18

TH Sung Eucharist

FR V611 B15, 108:1-5 TD 621 BD 641

P.M.

Ps. 65, 67. M 26 N 35

Ps. 93, 99 M 658 N 673

Ps. 24, 47. M 658 N 673

INDEX

A

Abba Father, 32, 34, 46, 82
Akiba, 48
Allegory, 32
Amen, 109
Aramaic, 25, 35, 98, 102, 104
Authenticity, 69, 72, 109

B

Babylon, 39
Bread, 112

C

Caesarea Philippi, 104
Carlyle, 112
Chinese religion, 63
Common prayer, 7
Communal purpose of Lord's
  Prayer, 25, 79

D

Daily bread, 96 f.
Dante, 113
David, 109
Debts, 100
Dependence, 5
Didaché, 30, 108
Doxology, 30

E

Early Christian prayers, 70
Egoism in prayer, 81
Egypt, 39
Eighteen Benedictions, 42, 61
Ending of Lord's Prayer, 25, 109
Epiousios, 98
Eternity in time, 118
Evil, physical and moral, 107
Evil One, 108

F

Faith, 13
"Father" in Jewish prayers, 48,
  64, 82
Forgiveness, 49, 99 f.
Fourth Gospel, 31, 90, 121
Futurity, 92 f.

G

Gethsemane, prayer in, 32, 95
Grace, sacramental, 114

H

Hallowing, 41, 86 f.
Hebrew religion, 88
Hebrews, Epistle to, 8, 31
High-priest, 86
Holiness, idea of, 87
Holy Spirit, 26, 70, 92

I

Importunity in prayer, 17
Individual prayer, 80 f.
Invocation, 85
Israel, 83, 89

J

James, Epistle of, 105
Jehovah, 86
Jewish prayers, 41 f.
John the Baptist, 30, 37, 79
Justification by faith, 10

K

Kaddish, 43, 91
Kingdom of God, 52, 64, 91 f.
Knowledge of God, 78

L

Last Supper, 97, 113